PUBLIC FINANCE AND OUR POVERTY

Owing to the antiquity and rarity of this book, certain pages are regrettably absent, and readability is compromised due to the blurring of the original text. If you possess any insights regarding the availability of these missing sections, kindly inform us. Your assistance is crucial in ensuring the completion of this significant work for the benefit of future generations.

PUBLIC FINANCE AND OUR POVERTY

The Contribution of Public Finance to the Present Economic state of India

BY

J. C. Kumarappa

Commendatory Foreword
BY

M. K. Gandhi

GYAN

Published by

GYAN

Gyan Publishing House
5, Ansari Road
Daryaganj, New Delhi-110002
Phone: 011-47034999, 9811692060
E-mail: books@gyanbooks.com

Distribution Network
gyanbooks.com
India, USA, Canada, UK, Australia

ISBN: 978-93-6208-805-5 (HB)
First Published, 1930

2nd Impression 2024

Printed at: Gyan Press, Delhi.

PUBLIC FINANCE AND OUR POVERTY
Author: J. C. KUMARAPPA

PUBLIC FINANCE AND OUR POVERTY

The Contribution of Public Finance to the Present Economic State of India

BY

J. C. Kumarappa

Commendatory Foreword
BY
M. K. Gandhi

NAVAJIVAN PUBLISHING HOUSE
AHMEDABAD

DEDICATED TO

Him who bears the burden and the heat of the day,

Whose extravagance consists in maintaining the most luxurious government in the world,

Whose generosity is in paying his taxes even at the cost of the subsistence of his wife and children,

And on whose shoulders the greatness of Great Britain rests.

"Thou shalt not muzzle the ox when he treadeth out the corn."

FOREWORD

This booklet is a reprint, revised where necessary by the author, of the chapters written by Professor Kumarappa and published in *Young India*. They examine the economic policy of the British Government and its effect upon the masses. They are, therefore, very seasonable. The value of the chapters is enhanced by the addition of a very careful and copious index prepared by the author himself. I commend the booklet both to the Indian as also the Western readers.

Karadi,
20th April, 1930 M. K. GANDHI

PREFACE TO THE THIRD EDITION

Though there has been no change in the circumstances cited in the first paragraph of the Preface to the Reprint of the Second Edition to warrant revision of the subject matter of this booklet, yet one more new device to exploit the finances of India has been forged by Great Britain in the last few years. This has called for an additional chapter on "Sterling Credits". With this exception the book remains but a reprint.

3rd July 1945
Wardha, C. P.

J. C. KUMARAPPA

PREFACE TO THE REPRINT OF THE SECOND EDITION

Circumstances have changed and events have occurred since the instances cited in the book had become history, but the policy of the British Government remains unchanged. India only exists to subserve the interests of Great Britain.

Time was when against the protests of the people railways were built to enable British steel interests to grow. Today, when the need of steel in Great Britain for war purposes is pressing, we witness hundreds of miles of the selfsame railroads being ripped up from the countryside growing wheat, oilseeds and cotton, and shipped to Great Britain leaving our farmers high and dry for lack of a satisfactory means of communication and transport.

The Railway workshops in India have thrown overboard the main object of their existence — to maintain the efficiency of the rolling stock and the permanent way — and have taken to the production of shell cases and other munitions of war, irrespective of the needs of the convenience and the safety of the public.

Even the efforts made to industrialize India today are confessedly for war purposes irrespective of the permanent nterests of the country.

Such instances, which prove that the real interests of the welfare of our country find no place in the consideration of the present Government, need not be multiplied or brought up-to-date. Hence the theme of the book stands though the scenes may change.

Although the last edition was out of print several years ago and the publishers had been pressing me to revise the book for another edition, pressure on my time has not made it possible for me to do so. The matter in the book, being more of historical facts than a discussion of current politics, can well afford to make a debut again after nearly a decade without being stale, and there being a continued demand for it, it is now being reprinted without any material change.

Wardha, C. P. J. C. KUMARAPPA
January 10, 1941

PREFACE TO THE SECOND EDITION

In bringing out a second edition of this booklet advantage is taken of the opportunity to add a chapter on "Public Debts". This chapter is mostly taken from a lecture given by me under the auspices of the Gujarat Sahitya Sabha at Ahmedabad. An appendix on the subject has also been added.

October, 1931 J. C. KUMARAPPA

PREFACE TO THE FIRST EDITION

Suggestions have been offered which indicate that the theme set forth in the title with the implications and limitations thereof has not been kept in mind by many readers.

May I state at the very outset that I am neither concerned with allocating responsibility nor with a comprehensive enquiry into the causes of poverty in India. This essay is merely an attempt to point out the injurious fiscal policies with the hope that good will result. I am, therefore, not concerned with all the circumstances which have impoverished the country, such as morcellement of land etc., however enchanting it may be to trace the economic course of the nation from the fabulous wealth of ancient India to the stigma of poverty now attaching to that very land. Although the changes in the environmental conditions which have brought these about are varied and fascinating, we cannot, within the scope of this booklet, get into such a maze, hence I have deliberately limited myself to only one such factor, *viz.* Public Finance.

Even in such a limited field we are not concerned with remote periods, but with the policies of an administration stretching over about a century prior to the present time. This historical aspect of the enquiry entails using evidence which may appear to be out of date. But it is well to remember that we are not dealing with present day policies only, but with past policies which have left their indelible marks on the economic condition of the people.

I have preferred also to judge by results and actions rather than by ostensible reasons advanced by Finance Members in an oratorial flourish. Because of this, I have refrained from dealing largely with present day affairs and have limited myself to tried policies of the past; for instance, my reference to the Excise Duty on cotton. In matters of this kind we can only go by what has been achieved and not merely by methods in use. It is no good pleading that a tax or an expenditure is good in itself. What we have to judge by is by the alternative. While there are pressing needs, if the revenue is used for less pressing objects however important or beneficial these latter may be in themselves, it is wrongly used. When children are starving, food and the means of obtaining food are more important than reading and writing, and the three R's are more important than a college education in a land of illiterates. It is futile to claim credit for building railways, good roads etc. We have to take into consideration at what 'alternative cost' these have been built and what use they are being put to and which part of the population benefits by them. If these are for the benefit of the foreign merchant, the plutocrat or the exploiter, to the neglect of the needs of the poor, it is a blot on the administration rather than a matter to be vaunted with legitimate pride.

Even this theme is too wide to be dealt with adequately in a booklet of this kind. Here it is only possible to indicate the main lines of inquiry. The method pursued is to present evidence and then corroborate the author's conclusions from accepted authorities.

As the figures used in the body of the essay relate to 1925/26 an Appendix has been added giving the latest available figures. Advantage has been taken of this to supplement other information as well, especially table IV of Appendix A will be found to be of great interest. France has always been considered a classic example of a stagnant population. When allowance is made for the territorial increase of British India during the last five decades, the reader will note that India 'takes the cake' even in this. So that increase in the density of the population does not supply a solution to the poverty of India as the Government protagonists will have us believe.

The material used in this essay was originally collected while I was a student under Prof. E. R. A. Seligman of Columbia University, New York, and was put together in a form suitable to the general reader and published as a series of articles in *Young India* during November, December 1929 and January 1930.

Gujarat Vidyapith,
Ahmedabad

J. C. KUMARAPPA

TABLE OF CONTENTS

I

INTRODUCTION

In the very beginnings of fiscal science in India, taxes were regarded as the remuneration of the kings for their services rendered to the people. The relations between the State and the people were based on contract, and thus public finance received recognition very early in Indian statecraft. Shukra says: "The king should enjoy fruits everywhere, but, at the same time, he should act like a slave in protecting his people."

Coming to modern times, we find, that there is hardly any other department of Government so closely related to the wellbeing of the nation, in the long run, as that of public finance. Indeed, when fiscal science is the handmaiden of public-spirited and far-sighted statesmen, it could be the making of a powerful nation, but when mishandled, it could also be the ruination of a flourishing people. Like all other powerful instruments, this science is equally capable of being used for good or ill, and therefore, it should be entrusted only to proved friends.

With its aid the Government should husband the natural resources of the land, as short-sighted private ownership might waste and exhaust them in a brief period of time. It is the function of the Government to take a long time view of affairs, as it could afford to wait, while individuals, in their anxiety to crowd into their span of three score years and ten as much of economic production as possible, are apt to ignore the waste their feverish activities may entail on the coming generations. In the United States of America forests of timber burnt down, both in clearing the ground for cultivation and in laying foundations for trunk roads, and the oil wells rapidly pumped out in competition, afford glaring examples of loss that may occur not only to one nation but to humanity at large, as the world has now become one whole economic web, and the loss to one part is a loss to all. Thus the present day fiscal science throws a heavy burden of responsibility on the shoulders of those who wield this weapon with such far-reaching consequences.

During the transitional periods, when nations pass from one stage to another, — agricultural to industrial, handicraft to factory system, — an efficient Government should guide the economic activity of the people into proper channels, so that the productivity of the nation may not suffer by the changes, but rather be increased by it, and that there may be no unnecessary waste in the switching over process. This may be done by wise expenditure on experimentation and dissemination of information so obtained, or by a well-conceived system of tariffs affording protection to infant industries against competition from highly organized foreign units, or by bounties meted out to encourage promising industries in their struggle at the commencement, or by subsidies helping out undertakings essential for national welfare. Such guidance, direction and help should result in a well-balanced proportion of various kinds of opportunities for the common people. The wellbeing of a nation does not depend on the monetary affluence of a few nor on the unlimited opportunities afforded to all by any one field of occupation; for the former will lead to a great inequality in distribution and to discontent, and the latter may spell disaster to the whole nation, as in the case of a drought upon an agricultural community. The nation that is allowed to run on a single track will soon find difficulties in supporting itself, production will not keep pace with the growth in population unless opportunities broaden out in proportion. A deeply interested Government can do a great deal in keeping a watchful eye on the tendencies of the times, in stimulating growth and checking signs of decay. A scientific combination of industries and commerce will lead to the wellbeing of the masses, and will result in their contentment and happiness in the enrichment of life to all individuals, rich and poor, high and low. Rightly does John Ruskin declare, "There is no wealth but life." J. A. Hobson suggests 'substituting for the monetary standard of wealth a standard of human wellbeing.' When we judge the profitableness of a Government policy, our criterion should be the provision of opportunities to all those who are willing to contribute their share of work and thought to the common good of the nation, that they may be able to do so freely with neither let nor hindrance.

The revenue of the king can be raised, says Shukra, only after he has contributed to the faculty of the people, like the gardener who collects the fruits and flowers after having duly nourished the plants. Taxation should be such that it does not hurt the populace. To use Kautilya's figure of speech, taxes should be obtained as the fruit is plucked when ripe without injury to the plant. The flock should be shorn and not flayed. A carefully devised system of taxes, while producing adequate revenue, should not reduce the productivity of the tax-payer; the revenue should be drawn from the surplus without affecting the patrimony of the State. To again borrow an ancient Hindu simile, the State should not be like a charcoal dealer who cuts down the trees, burns them, and obtains a profit at the cost of the destruction of the source of revenue, but it should be like the florist who merely gathers the flowers which would otherwise fade, leaving the plant to bloom again. The incidence of taxation should be carefully considered, and the burden should be according to faculty. Those on the borderland of subsistence should be relieved at the cost of those who are blessed with a larger share of worldly goods. Indirect taxes should be levied only on articles carefully and scientifically selected, so that indigenous industries are encouraged and the poorer classes are not crushed by a higher cost of living owing to the taxes pushing up the prices of necessaries. Indirect taxes are very useful means of obtaining revenue without making the one, who ultimately bears the burden, aware of it. Hindu literature likens it to the process by which the bees suck the honey without the flowers knowing it. This quality in its nature calls for the exercise of great caution on the part of those who are entrusted with this high duty.

The laying out of the revenue so obtained should be such as to increase the productivity of the people. To use a classical figure, the taxes should rise as the vapour from the sea, from the section of the populace who could best pay, and should be precipitated like rain on the needy, as when the rich are taxed to pay for the education of the poor. Even in private economy it requires a great deal more wisdom to spend the money well than to acquire it. The problem is far more complicated in public finance. It would be sheer folly to extract a rupee from a man on the subsistence level, to whom that unit represents great marginal utility, and to spend it so as to afford benefit to one who is much better off. There would be a waste of national income rupee for rupee. The faculty of the community from which the tax is raised and the utility to the group that benefits from the fund has to be always borne in mind.

The administration itself should be as efficient as the nation can afford to maintain, taking into consideration the economic development of the people. It would be reasonable for a man with an income of Rs. 6,000 a year to aspire to a 'Ford', if his family is not too numerous even for that, but it would be madness for him to maintain a 'Rolls Royce'. The standards of efficiency required are relative and not absolute. There should be a sense of proportion in all things including even public administration. It is no argument to maintain a very highly paid administration to say that it is efficient. Efficiency itself should be gauged, not by the mechanical accuracy with which routine work is carried out, but on the touchstone of prosperity of the general mass of the people. Mechanical efficiency should be subordinated to the need for imagination in carving out wide channels for the exercise of national talents. An administration that does not lead to such prosperity is a failure, however efficient it may be in its clockwork detail. To weigh up the ability of a nation to maintain the expense of its administration, the salaries of its public servants should be tied up to a multiple of the average income of a citizen for comparison. Such a procedure will give the proper proportion, and at the same time will automatically eliminate the difference in price levels between countries compared, and the faculty of different citizens.

With these general remarks on the prerequisites for the building up of a wealthy nation in mind, we shall rapidly review the conditions prevailing in India. To get an adequate perspective to enable us to trace the influence of the policies of public finance pursued in India, it will be necessary to survey briefly the economic state of the country, immediately preceding the present regime, leaving aside ancient India which bore the magnificence of the empires of Chandragupta' Ashoka etc.

II

INDIA ABOUT 1800

Although for centuries past Indian history alternated with prosperity and adversity, peace and war, contentment and oppression, benevolence and tyranny, on the whole, when we look at the general trend, we find India enjoyed a remarkable share of peace and prosperity as compared with the lot of the other nations of those days. All through mediaeval times, India occupied the centre of the economic activity of the world. Even the discovery of America was due to the eagerness with which the less developed nations of the West were seeking to get into direct trade relations with India. According to the standards then prevailing, India was highly industrialized. Foreign trade in those days consisted of small articles of great value, usually of the luxury type, exchanged for gold. As security and transport played an important part in the cost and transfer of goods, it was not worth while to exchange for bulky and low-priced raw materials. Even Rome, in its height of power, complained of the drain of gold to India. No doubt the belief, that India is an incorrigible consumer of the precious metals, which persists to this day in spite of evidences to the contrary, had its origin in the manner in which India's foreign trade was paid for in ancient times. India was exporting manufactured articles and importing gold in exchange in the main. Her own raw materials were worked up by her own skilled artisans, and Indian[1] bottoms carried the wares to Europe, via the Persian Gulf and Arabia, on the one side and to China and Japan on the other. Thus she was a veritable hive of activity, affording profitable employment to her sons on land, on sea and in her cities. She had an admirable combination of outlets for the genius of her people. Her cotton was skilfully woven into beautiful calicoes of Calicut on the western coast and into fine

1. Radhakumud Mookerji's *A History of Indian Shipping*, page 4.

muslins of Musulipatam along the Eastern seaboard. The trade in such fabrics with England, in the latter part of the 18th century, assumed such proportions,[1] that it raised a hue and cry for protective tariff against Indian competition. The following lines which appeared in the *Gentleman's Magazine* in 1735 give some indication of the keenness of the competition of the Indian trade in England:

> "The silkworms form the wardrobes' gaudy pride:
> How rich the vest which Indian looms provide;
> Yet let me here the British Nymphs advise
> To hide these foreign spoils from native eyes;
> Lest rival artists murmuring for employ
> With savage rage the envied work destroy."

Heavy duties were introduced[2] in England to safeguard British textile manufacturers from utter ruin. Cunningly wrought works of art in ivory and precious stones were in great demand everywhere, and the spices of Ind became proverbial. Silks, embroidery, and carpets catered to the aesthetic demands of the wealthy.

The great maritime activity led to shipbuilding. Prof. Radhakumud Mookerji quotes from a letter, dated 16th December 1670, from the factors at Balasore to the Court of Directors in London, the following[3]: "Many English merchants and others have their ships and vessels yearly built. Here is the best and well-grown timber, in sufficient plenty, the best iron upon the coast; any sort of iron work is here ingeniously performed by the natives, as spikes, bolts, anchors and the like. Very expert master builders there are several here; they build very well and launch with as much discretion as I have seen in any part of the world. They have an excellent way of making shrouds, stays, and any other rigging for the ships." Even[4] as late as 1802 ships and warships for England were built by India, and England borrowed[5] plans and designs from Indian builders.

1. Balkrishna's *Commercial Relations between England and India*, Chap. X.
2. Wm. Digby's '*Prosperous*' *British India*, page 90.
3. Radhakumud Mookerji's *A History of Indian Shipping*, page 233.
4. *Ibid*, page 244.
5. *Ibid*, page 250.

The beautiful buildings and canals as well as the public trunk roads, constructed during this period and existing to this day, bear eloquent testimony to the prosperity of the times.

It is true, famines devastated the country in parts, but never the whole land, at any one time. The chief cause was mainly the shortage of grain following a drought, not the lack of purchasing power. It was a natural calamity rather than the result of the economic situation. Owing to the inadequate facilities of those days transport was both slow and arduous, making relief[1] work an almost insuperable difficulty.

From time to time some foreign ruler would cast his envious eyes on the wealth of India, descend on the country and carry off the hoarded treasures of the temples and palaces. A certain amount of loot by predatory armies was inevitable by the nature of events, but on the whole the 'underlying' population of peasants and artisans were allowed to carry on their respective avocations in peace. At all events, the means of wealth creation was not taken away from them by the invasion, and the people were left free to engage in production again. If, indeed, the wealth of a nation, taken as a whole, depends on the productivity of that nation, and not on the monetary accumulation, then we can safely say that those inroads little interfered with the welfare of the people. Farming was looked upon as sacred, and warring princes scrupulously avoided any destruction or damage to agricultural property. It is easy to understand how an invasion such as that of Nadir Shah in 1739 need not cause untold misery by destroying the economic unity of the nation, though it may bring about a temporary disturbance. We can conceive of America losing the wealth of a Rockfeller or of a Ford without much hardship to the nation; but it would indeed be a sad plight if the livelihood of the farmers and the openings for employment of the labouring classes in industrial areas were taken away. 'He who steals my purse steals trash.'

1. A. Loveday's *History and Economics of Indian Famines*, page 20.

Comparatively little injury is done if a man is robbed but is left with the means of supporting himself; on the other hand, if a skilled worker is robbed, his eyes put out, and his hands cut off, his condition is indeed miserable. Foreign invasions and tyrannical reigns did oppress the people for a while, but it was not long before the road to welfare was regained.

Whether well or ill, the proceeds of taxation was spent in the land. The extravagances of the courts only went to encourage arts and crafts, as it meant a greater demand for the products of these. Eastern princes were well known for their patronage of scholars and artists. The nation as a whole benefited by its own total productivity. What it produced it consumed without having to hand over a share to an outsider. The administration itself being manned by the sons of the soil, the doors of public service were thrown open to the able amongst the intellectual classes, besides providing occupation for thousands of others.

Village lands were assessed by their own panchayats who had intimate personal knowledge of the locality and of the tax-payer. Although the tax rates appeared high, the human element and the personal touch in the government often led to bargaining and relief. The tax itself was based on the produce and so was proportionate. An option to pay the tax either in kind or in money was extended to the farmers, thus supplying the needed safety valve to hardships that may be entailed otherwise. A surplus was available to the farmers and others as reserves[1] of grain against drought. The land was not swept clean of all its production, without laying aside a margin of safety.

Each village had its own school[2] supported by land grants, and it had its own officers in charge of the various departments[3] of local government, thus constituting a little democratic unit.

The following accounts from European travellers and observers of the conditions at the time in the North, South,

1. A. Loveday's *History and Economics of Indian Famines*, page 21.
2. J. Matthai's *Village Government in British India*, Chap. II.
3. *Ibid*, page 15.

East and West sections of the country, give us a picture of a flourishing country at the end of the 18th century.

Bishop Heber describes Bharatpur State in his journal, and says, "This country[1] . . . is one of the best cultivated and watered tracts which I have seen in India. The crops of corn on the ground were really beautiful; that of cotton . . . . a very good one. ·What is sure proof of wealth, I saw several sugar mills, and large pieces of ground where the cane had just been cleared. The population did not seem great, but the villages were in good condition and repair, and the whole afforded so pleasing a picture of industry and was so much superior to anything I had been led to expect in Rajputana, which I had seen in the Company's territories, that I was led to suppose that either the Raja of Bharatpur was an extreme exemplary and paternal governor, or that the system of management adopted in the British provinces was less favourable to the improvement and happiness of the country than some of the Native States."

Another witness, Lt.-Col. Moore, bears the following testimony of the Musalman Prince Tippu of Mysore in the South: "When[2] a person, travelling through a strange country finds it well cultivated, populous with industrious inhabitants, cities well founded, commerce extending, towns increasing and everything flourishing so as to indicate happiness, he naturally concludes the form of Government congenial to the people. This is a picture of Tippu's Govenment. . . . We have reason to suppose his subjects to be happy as those of any other sovereign . . . No murmurings or complaints were heard against him, though the enemies of Tippu were in power, and would have been gratified by any aspersions on his character."

Turning to the East, we get this description of Bengal from Mr. Holwell:[3] "Here the property as well as the

1. Bishop Heber's Journal, Vol II, page 17.

2. From Moore's *Narrative of the War with Tippu Sultan*, page 201 (quoted from the Reform Pamphlet by Lajpat Rai).

3. Lajpat Rai's *England's Debt to India*, page 25.

liberty of the people are inviolable. The traveller with or without merchandise becomes the immediate care of the Government, which allots him guards, without any expense, to conduct him from stage to stage." And again: "The rich province of Dacca was cultivated in every part. . . . Justice was administered impartially. . . . Jaswant Roy . . . had been educated in purity, integrity and indefatigable attention to business, and studied to render the government of his province conducive to the general ease and happiness of his people. He abolished all monopolies and imposts upon grain."

Regarding the West, Anqetil du Perron observes the Mahratta country and says: "When I entered the country of the Mahrattas, I thought myself in the midst of simplicity and happiness of the golden age, where nature was as yet unchanged, and war and misery were unknown. The people were cheerful, vigorous and in high health, and unbounded hospitality was an universal virtue; every door was open and friends, neighbours and strangers were alike welcome to whatever they found."

From these pleasing pictures of a prosperous country at the beginning of the 19th century, let us turn to the state of India at the beginning of the next century.

III

INDIA ABOUT 1900

Let us again put into the witness-box a few European observers. We can well begin with no less a person than the Premier of England, Mr. J. Ramsay MacDonald, who says, "For[1] days and days one goes through the land, and sees nothing but thin bodies toiling, toiling, trudging, trudging, trudging. India is the home of the poverty-stricken, and this was borne in upon me all the more that its poverty was embodied in forms of the most perfect human grace." And later he declares: "The poverty[2] of India is not an opinion, it is a fact."

Dr. Josiah Oldfield writes to the *Daily News* as follows: "I have[3] just returned from a study of the Indian problems on the spot, and cannot urge too earnestly before your readers the intense pathos of seeing village after village, village after village with all the men, still more the women and children, showing those pitiful signs of a daily struggle to live, with only half enough to live upon.

"I have seen the poverty of the English villages, and the desolation of the London slums (and a doctor in the slums sees more of the real poverty of the homes than a person does), but I have seen nothing that haunts me more than the spectacle of these brave, honest, hardworking, economical people toiling on week after week, with only a piece of coarse *bajri* or *jovari* bread and a handful of pickles to keep it down, and a drink of butter-milk twice a day.

"There is no declared famine in India at the present time (1902), but I have visited scores of villages, and have entered many a house, and have found the corn bin empty or nearly empty.

"What does this mean? It means that their scanty harvest has already been sold to pay the tax, and that in another two months they will have nothing at all left."

---

1. J. R. MacDonald's *The Awakening of India*, page 140.
2. *Ibid*, page 159.
3. Wm. Digby's *The Ruining of India*, page 159.

The Rev. J. Knowles,[1] of the London Missionary Society, witnesses: "In my own missionary experience, I once carefully investigated the earnings of a congregation of 300, and found the average amounted to less than a farthing a head per day. They did not live; they eked out an existence."

Prof. Gilbert Slater of London pronounces[2] the poverty of India as a 'grim fact'.

As recently as 1927 Dr. Rutherford observed, that 'everywhere'[3] the struggle for existence was terrible, and after describing the privations the villagers suffered, he goes on to say: "Perhaps my greatest horror and anguish arose from the facts, firstly, that I was a British citizen, was responsible for their physical condition leading to a slow and painful death, inasmuch as I was responsible for the Government which failed to prevent famines by greater schemes of irrigation and by reducing the assessment on land."

The economist, H. M. Hyndman, opines:[4] "Even as we look on, India is becoming feebler and feebler, the very lifeblood of the great multitude under our rule is slowly, yet ever faster, ebbing away."

Leaving the bird's-eye-view of affairs obtained from these snapshots, let us examine the situation at closer range. We find the old-time skilled handicraftsmen and artisans have lost their trade, and no industry has replaced them, but these men have been driven back to the land to eke out a precarious living with a slightly increased population. Part of the year they work, but when the dry season sets in, they are left idle.

The relative increase in population during the last century is very much lower in India than it has been in Europe. According to the *Statesman's Year Book* the percentage increase during the last three decades, as revealed by

1. Wm. Digby's *'Prosperous' British India*, page 106.
2. P. Pillai's *Economic Conditions in India*, page XII.
3. V. H. Rutherford's *Modern India*, page 106.
4. H. M. Hyndman's *Bankruptcy of India*, page 152.

the census, compares with that in Great Britain as follows:

	1891-1901	1901-1911	1911-1921
India	2·5	1·7	1·2
Great Britain	12·2	11·6	5·4

So the increase in population does not cause a problem[1].

We observe the foreign trade of the country has changed from an export of manufactured articles to an import of such merchandise, and an export of raw materials. The cotton textiles as a cottage industry have disappeared, leaving nothing to take their place. Shipping and ship-building is as a tale that is told.

We notice there has been a large number of famines[2], and these more devastating ones in the last half a century than throughout the past of India's long history. The range of distribution of wealth is immense.

Everywhere the administration appears to be practically in the hands of European officers who naturally work with their return passage in their pockets. Their interests are not identified with the interests of those whom they govern, nor are they responsible to them. Their feet indeed rest on Indian soil, but their faces are turned *Homewards*. The sons of the soil who were once the administrators have been reduced to an ill-paid community of clerks.

'The[3] widespread system of national education,' which the British found when they took possession of the country, met the fate of the other indigenous institutions with the taxing of school lands.

We find a highly efficient and well developed network of railways, but comparatively little spent on canals and irrigation.

India is 'enjoying a free-trade policy' as regards her foreign connections, while the requisite revenue is raised from salt monopoly, land tax and other regressive taxation.

It is for us now to enquire what has happened, in so short a period in a nation's life, to transform the glowing picture of the early 19th century into the harrowing tales of the 20th century.

1. For further elucidation see Appendix A. § IV.
2. A. Loveday's *History and Economics of Indian Famines*, App. A.
3. John Matthai's *The Village Government in British India*, page 42.

The conditions that affect a nation's welfare may be broadly divided into:

1. Those inherent in man, and
2. Those due to environment,
(a) natural, and (b) artificial.

As regards the inherent qualities of the Indian ryot, his intelligence and diligence and his powers of endurance under the most trying and disheartening circumstances have never been called into question, so this can be dismissed with the evidence of the illustrious labour leader of England. Mr. MacDonald is of the opinion, that "the people[1] are the most industrious in the world, much of their land is fertile and yields rich crops."

When we turn to the natural environment, we find that there are very few countries as richly endowed as India is. The hidden treasure trove consists of manganese, copper, iron, coal, gold, petroleum, salt, lead and lead ores, saltpetre etc. The soil offers tea, coffee, indigo, and India holds the world monopoly of jute and third place for cotton. Wheat and oilseed form other important products for world markets. The many lofty mountain ranges hold potentialities for the generation of electric power. With such manifold blessings India can plead no excuse under this head for her dire poverty. Thus man and nature stand acquitted, and so we pass on to the next.

Dealing with the theory that production is low because the standard of living is low, Dr. H. J. Davenport says: "Men[2] do not stop consuming because they want no more goods, but because they can get no more on terms that make this more worth while." What are these factors in India that make 'this more' not worth while? Owing to the limitation of our theme we shall confine ourselves to one of the chief factors among the many artificial environments, namely, Public Finance. In India, governmental policies control also railways and foreign exchange, which will, therefore, come under our purview.

---

1. J. R. MacDonald's *The Awakening of India*, page 159.
2. H. J. Davenport's *Economics of Enterprise*, page 2.

The main difference in approach between public finance and private finance is due to the fact that the individual has a fixed source of income, and he has to regulate his expenditure according to his means, but in the case of governments, the amount to be spent on various purposes is decided upon, and then they look around for ways and means of raising the wherewithal to meet such expenditure. Hence, we shall first take up the consideration of expenditure, and then examine the means by which the revenue is raised.

Although a Government may appear to have the advantage, in that it can control, at least in theory, the revenue to meet its needs, we should not lose sight of the fact that such power is not absolute but only relative to the faculty of the people, which in reality limits the taxation that a nation can bear. The moment the incidence passes from the surplus to luxuries, a certain amount of resistance is encountered which becomes greater and greater as we get down the scale of incomes from luxuries to comforts, and from comforts to necessaries. In the nature of things, when the income, barely sufficient to support the worker in a state of efficiency, is taxed, the faculty of the people is at an end, and any further increase in taxation can only result in damaging the patrimony of the State. It is inevitable, that any system of taxation must mean hardship to a few, as it is hardly possible for human ingenuity to devise a means of measuring individual ability to pay. But great care can be taken to see that efficiency does not suffer, and as far as possible, incomes on the subsistence level are exempt from any burden.

Under these conditions, having ascertained the amount available, the revenue should be expended so as to obtain the best possible value for every rupee of public money. Expenditure which will increase the productivity of the masses should be preferred to such as will benefit only a class; administration expenses should always be kept down.

As Government revenue is only a slice off the national income, it should be returned to the people in the form of expenditure on their behalf; any amount not so returned impoverishes them, as they do not get the full benefit of their production.

IV

PUBLIC EXPENDITURES

The following figures of net expenditure, prepared from the Statistical Abstract for the fiscal year 1925-26, including both Central and Provincial Governments, are instructive as to the use the available resources are put to:

Debt Services	21,62,09,009	15.2
Military	55,99,85,654	39.5
Civil Administration	55,44,33,587	39.2
Miscellaneous	8,70,60,535	6.1
	Rs. 141,76,88,785	100.0

The details of 'Civil Administration' are as follows:

	Lakhs	Per Cent
General Administration	12,49	8.9
Audit	84	.58
Justice	4,69	3.31
Jails	1,94	1.38
Police	11,69	8.2
Ports	31	.21
Ecclesiastical	32	.22
Political	3,37	2.4
Scientific	86	.6
Education	10,66	7.6
Medical	3,20	2.28
Public Health	1,81	1.25
Agriculture	1,79	1.24
Industries	1,30	.92
Aviation & Miscellaneous	17	.11
	55,44	39.20

At this stage it will be useful to compare, with the above, the functional distribution of expenditure in the

United States of America for the same year, including Federal, State and Local:

	Millions	Per Cent
[1]Debt Services	2,432	22.3
Protection	2,085	18.7
Central Government	867	7.8
Education	2,167	19.5
Highways	1,568	14.1
Social Welfare	1,020	9.1
Public Utilities	583	5.2
Economic Development	207	1.9
Miscellaneous	155	1.4
	11,134	100.0

We should remember, that the above [2]figures represent the utilization of the revenue of a democratic country controlling its own finances, while in India there is no such popular control. Again owing to the difference in the classification of expenditures in the two countries, it is not possible to press the comparison too closely, but we can discern a wide variation in the policies of the two governments, and more especially when we remember that 'Protection' in America includes 'Police' also, and their combatant forces are much better paid than are those of other nations.

While America spends 48.8% on Debts, Military and General Governmental Expenditures, and the balance in nation building expenses led by Education with 19.5% India spends 93.7% on Debts, Military and Administrative Expenses and so has very little left for developmental purposes. Even out of the little used for Education, the Government of India spends Rs. 25 per head of the European population in India on the education of the children of the Europeans; while it doles out a beggarly four annas per head of the children of the land, which is one hundredth of what it utilizes for the education of the children of [3]Europeans in

1. See Appendix § III.
2. *The Cost of Government of the United States*, page 18.
3. Lajpat Rai's *Unhappy India*, pages 55-56.

India. Is this nation building expenditure in the interests of the 'people committed to its charge'? Only the crumbs are thrown to the sons of the soil in India, under the present fiscal system.

DEBT SERVICES AND MILITARY EXPENDITURES

Prof. K. T. Shah has worked out the following percentages[1] of Total Expenditure that the various countries spend on 'Defence':

India	63.8	Spain	17.6
United Kingdom	53.7	France	20.0
Australia	48.3	Italy	17.3
Canada	24.2	United States	38.2
S. Africa	5.2	Japan	49.0

These figures relate to the year 1922, but they give us an idea of how India is being burdened with unproductive expenditures. When the nation gets no return for its effort, will this not be sufficient in itself to reduce a country to poverty in the course of years? The unproductive[2] debts were mainly incurred by the British in conquering India itself, and in financing wars of imperial interests in Asia and Africa, leaving India to pay the bill. In addition, India's 'trustees' made a 'gift' to themselves of one hundred million pounds during the World War, while at that time India suffered losses, computed by Prof. Shah[3] to be 180 crores. As these enormous debts were incurred in quarrels not her own, and in pursuit of interests not identical with hers, it is hardly fair to saddle India with these charges.

As regards the maintenance of the Army itself, after arguing the various needs of the country, Prof. Shah says: "The[4] Army in India is thus as expensive as it is useless; and the service alleged to be rendered by that instrument to the Indian people is clearly out of all proportion to its cost."

---

1. K. T. Shah's *Wealth and Taxable Capacity of India*, page 267.
2. See Ch. VI on "Public Debts" and Appendix E. § I.
3. K. T. Shah's *Wealth and Taxable Capacity of India*, page 276.
4. *Ibid.* page 272.

Ramsay MacDonald comes to rather similar conclusion when he says: "Undoubtedly[1] India has not been dealt with fairly in this respect." "A[2] large part of the army in India — certainly [3]one half — is an Imperial Army which we require for other than purely Indian purposes, and its costs, therefore, should be met from Imperial and not Indian Funds."

CIVIL ADMINISTRATION

We find this item is about five times as expensive as in the United States, and it is no wonder that Mr. MacDonald confesses: "It[4] must be admitted that the Government of India is an expensive affair," and later on adds: "A foreign[5] government is always a dear government—even if it is worth its price."

India competes for its administrators in Great Britain, a country of high price level; therefore, the scale of salaries must, necessarily, be high enough to be an attraction. Furthermore, foreign service involves a certain amount of 'human cost' which has to be compensated by a still higher remuneration. In the early days of British rule, when the British system of government was foreign and novel, there may have been some excuse for importing raw youths from England for fat jobs which afforded them fine careers, but now with tens of thousands of Indians educated in Western methods, this system has no particle of justification. The bureaucracy has been lacking in imagination and initiative of late. The work runs in deep grooves, and they have done little to increase the productivity of the nation. [6]In 1913,

1. J. R. MacDonald's *The Government of India*, page 153.
2. *Ibid*, page 154.
3. See Appendix E § II.
4. J. R. MacDonald's *The Government of India*, page 145.
5. *Ibid*, page 147.
6. Although there has been an increase in the Indian element in the services since 1913, yet for purposes of our illustration it makes little difference, as the main plea is not for Indianization but for allocating a larger share for nation building purposes such as education etc., and not using up any amounts so allotted merely in paying large salaries to officials of the departments.

of the posts[1] carrying Rs. 1,000 and over per month 96% were held by Europeans and Anglo-Indians and only 4% by Indians. Taking the whole service, the average pay of a post held by an Indian was Rs. 371. When we compare these amounts with the *per capita* income,—Rs. 50 *per*[2] *annum* in 1911—of the taxpayer, who pays for this service, we see, one European official is equivalent to 224 taxpayers and an Indian official to 84 taxpayers. It is obvious that both European and Indian officials are paid far too high a salary when we take the faculty of the people into consideration. New York, the richest State in the richest country, pays its Governor $. 10,000 a year, about 14 times the average income of a citizen; while Bombay pays its Governor Rs. 1,20,000 ($. 45,000), about 2,400 times the income of the average taxpayer. Ramsay MacDonald dealing with this question suggests[3]: "Every branch of public service should have as its standard of pay an Indian and not a foreign level," and admits,[4] "Thus far we have wrought India much harm, and this is a reform which a self-government would do well to make."

Apart from the fact that a large portion of the revenue is thus absorbed by the administration,—leaving very little for anything else,—if the personnel had been Indian, a good deal of the wealth would have merely changed hands and would not have affected very much the country as a whole. The fact, that a large amount of the country's production goes into the hands of these foreign administrators and a considerable portion of it is drained out of the country in savings and pensions, is a matter of great concern to those who are interested in the welfare of India. Referring to pensions, J. Ramsay MacDonald says:[5] "And these dead charges under a foreign government are doubly serious, for they are not only drawn from Indian production but are

1. K. T. Shah's ***Sixty Years of Indian finance***, page 101.
2. G. F. Shirras, ***Bombay Working Class Budget***, page 11.
3. J. R. MacDonald's ***The Government of India***, page 147.
4. ***Ibid***, page 148.
5. ***Ibid***, page 148.

withdrawn from India itself." And he goes on to add:[1] "It withdraws from a fertilizing stream a very considerable amount of necessary water, and means impoverishment." And he finally states:[2] "Prosperity cannot be widespread if the exported tribute is heavy."

Thus we see that 93.9% of the expenditure only depletes production, the bulk of it going out of the country in return for very little. As the productivity of the people is not increased thereby, and they do not get the full return for their efforts, the continuance of such a policy, decade after decade, is bound to reduce any country to poverty.

CAPITAL EXPENDITURE

The outlay under this head should be in proper relation to the needs of the economic development of the country. However good an item may be in itself, if the interests of the country do not call for it, it remains a waste. A country like India urgently needs developmental expenditure on irrigation and cheap rural transportation. While the Government has spent 96 crores on irrigation, the amount spent on railways to the end of 1925-26 is 626 crores.[3] India has the largest mileage of railways in Asia,—38,579 miles. Ignoring the other pressing needs, railway construction was pushed on, exhausting all the available resources in doing so. The reason for this is clear from the following quotation: "But,[4] from the borrowed capital, railway and other works were executed which were devised in War Offices and not in Counting Houses, and Military Expenditure became masked as railway development," says Mr. MacDonald.

Apart from the military aspect, this policy also helped to keep the steel industries in Great Britain busy. The railways were further useful in bringing raw materials to the ports for shipment to England, and carrying inland manufactured articles from abroad by utilizing discriminating[5]

1. J. R. MacDonald's *The Government of India*, page 148.
2. *Ibid*, page 149.
3. *The Statistical Abstract of British India*, page 217.
4. J. R. MacDonald's *The Government of India*, page 151.
5. N. B. Mehta's *Indian Railways: Rates & Regulations*, pages 134-5.

rates and 'block rates'. To cite only a few instances to show how this scheme was worked out in practice, let us first take an infant industry, like the match industry; the rate for imported matches from Bombay to Delhi was the same as the rate for locally made matches from Ahmedabad to Delhi although the latter is a shorter haul by three hundred miles. This was virtually "a bounty[1] to the foreign manufacturer equivalent to the whole cost of carriage from Bombay to Ahmedabad." After a continued agitation of about ten years by the manufacturers of Ahmedabad, the rates were reduced to Rs. 2-2-11 per maund from Ahmedabad and to Rs. 3-7-2 from Bombay.

If we turn to an indigenous industry, like sugar manufacture, we find, the rate from Bombay to Cawnpore for imported *refined* sugar is as. 13-6 per maund for the 840 miles, while for indigenous sugar from Cawnpore to Akola, a distance of only 649 miles, the rate is Rs. 1-2-4 per maund. This discrimination becomes still more unjust when we remember that the imported article is high-priced, while the country manufactured stuff is low-priced, and under the principle of charging 'what the traffic will bear,' the former should bear the heavier rate. Again, *refined* sugar from Bombay to Barsi is as. 6 per maund, while *unrefined* jaggery, used by the poor people, from Barsi to Bombay is charged at as. 9-9 per maund, *i. e.*, over 50% higher. Sjt. Mehta remarks,[2] "Not only were the lower rates offered to foreign sugar as against home made sugar, but even as against *gud* or jaggery—a much less valuable product and largely consumed by the impecunious masses."

As an instance of preference given to industries run by Europeans in India we may cite the discrimination in rates between Delhi, an Indian centre of cotton industries, and Cawnpore, a European centre of cotton industries. The rate from Chaudani to Cawnpore, a distance of 236 miles, is as. 5 per maund for raw cotton; but to Delhi, a distance of only 128 miles, it is as. 6-7 per maund. Sjt.

1. N. B. Mehta's *Indian Railways: Rates & Regulations*, page 149.
2. *Ibid*, page 149.

Mehta states[1] that, "this discriminative treatment resulted in closing down of some cotton mills at Delhi."

Similar facilities in rates are given to raw hides, wheat etc. to the ports as against the rates to centres of Indian manufacture. Sjt. Ghose describes such rate discrimination 'as a subsidy[2] paid by the Indian Government to foreign manufacturer.'

While none will deny the advantages to be derived from the possession of rapid means of transport, it has to be conceded that India has been overloaded by a system far in excess of its needs at the present economic state. Usually railway development follows economic demands; but in India, it is considerably in advance, and hence it is unable to pay for itself, with the result that large amounts of Government revenue have to be diverted to maintain these unnatural and parasitic growths. Besides, the manner in which an effective instrument is used will determine the advantages to be derived from it. From the samples given above, it is clear that railways have not been an unmixed blessing to India. While we have a very limited amount of capital available, that amount has been lavishly expended in building railways to the neglect of the more important construction of canals for irrigation and transport, sanitation works etc. The Government cannot plead that the excessive development was due to an 'error of judgment', as it is not the outcome of a moment's hasty decision, but of a policy persistently followed, decade after decade, in the teeth of continued public criticism.

Discriminating rates are nothing new in railway history throughout the world. In the United States and other countries private enterprise and greed was the cause of it while, in India, the damaging part lies in the fact, that the railways are aided and controlled by a Government which holds itself forth as a 'trustee', and hence its action amounts to a criminal neglect of its duty to the Indian taxpayer.

---

1. N. B. Mehta's ***Indian Railways: Rates & Regulations***, page 149.
2. ***Lectures on Indian Railway Economics***, part II, page 36.

The famous financier, D. E. Wachha, expresses himself as[1] follows: "It is the permanent Indian population of the country which directly or indirectly bears the whole burden of the annually growing charge on Railway Public Debt. If any interests require to be consulted, it is the interests of this permanent tax-paying population and not the interests of a handful of foreign exploiters here today and gone tomorrow, who deem India to be their happy hunting ground. It is an altogether inexcusable railway policy which is eager to attend to the interests of this microscopic class, but which absolutely ignores the millions of the indigenous population. In short, as in many other matters, so in connection with railways, it is the foreign exploiter who calls the tune, but it is the indigenous taxpayer who is called upon to pay the piper."

William Digby[2] writes, "Railways have facilitated the transfer of produce from one part of the country to another, but they have not increased production; they have carried produce out of the country, but, . . . only a small portion of the profits thus obtained have inured to the benefit of the native inhabitant of India, whilst a large portion of them are a veritable curse to the country. More and more produce and manufactures are needed to meet the ever growing charges in England, partly for railways, the same railways have facilitated the carriage of such products to the detriment and the ruin of the country."

While the trunk lines to the ports have been so well developed, the light railways and canal traction, which are so important for the betterment of rural economy, have been sadly neglected.[3] The Government has yielded to the importunities of the several British Chambers of Commerce, and failed to listen to the still small voice of the Indian people.

A certain proportion of the responsibility for the frequency of the occurrence of famines in India in the

1. D. E. Wachha's *Indian Railway Finance*, page 60.
2. William Digby's *The Ruining of India*, page 9.
3. Radhakamal Mukerji's *The Rural Economy of India*, page 226.

recent past has to be allocated to the rapid development of railways. The country has been drained of its reserves of food grains for distant markets. It is true, railways have also been instrumental in relieving famine areas by rushing food grains from provinces of plenty: this is a remedy. Prevention lies in conserving available resources which, owing to the pressure of taxation, the ryots are obliged to dispose of, and the cheaper railway transport aids the foreign agent who, in many cases, buys up the crops even before they are ready for harvest. In addition to this drain, the scarcity thus caused further pushes up the prices.

Thus we see that enormous amounts have been spent in building railways, largely for military purposes, and even in so far as commercial interests were taken into consideration, they were influenced by foreign merchants and manufacturers. The policies have not centred round the Indian taxpayer, nor have they materially added to his production. What funds were available were sunk in this enterprise which had to be subsidized, as the economic requirements of the country did not call for such an elaborate development.

Besides the sinking of the capital in railways not calculated to ameliorate the conditions of the poor, further capital expenditures have been devised to dispose of the available meagre balance in other ways equally unproductive, and useless so far as the wellbeing of the masses was concerned. H. M. Hyndman records "The foreign[1] Government has become even more expensive, and extravagances such as the creation of new and wholly unnecessary capital cities at Delhi and Dacca encourage waste to the extent of many millions sterling. Naturally to keep pace with this fatal system, the land tax is more cruelly exacted than ever, and the agriculturists get poorer all the time."

Should we look upon equalizing of distribution as one of the purposes of Government expenditures, we see that the fiscal system of India fails even here. A large proportion

1. H. M. Hyndman's *The Truth about India*, page 43.

of the disbursements is made in Great Britain and never returns to the taxpayer at all. Indeed the vapour rises from the starving millions of India and precipitates and refreshes the comparatively wealthy population of an island 5,000 miles away. Prof. Shah estimates[1], that out of the total tax collection of 400 crores, nearly 200 crores never bring any real return to the people of India, including 'the Home Charges,' *i. e.,* the Sterling commitments of the Secretary of State for India, over which the Government of India has no control.

Paper Currency and Exchange

Again in its currency policy, the Government is not concerned with the stability of the purchasing power of the rupee which affects the welfare of the people, but with the maintenance of the stability of the rupee in terms of the sovereign to meet the interests of those engaged in foreign trade. To this end it maintains the foreign exchange by means of the Gold Exchange Standard Reserve and keeps this reserve of 40 millions and a paper currency reserve of 20 millions in bullion and securities in London. This amount represents a loanable capital of over six hundred crores of which India, which stands greatly in need of industrial development, is deprived, as the clamours of the London bankers are more easily heard. If ever there was a need for the expansion of industrial banking, it is now, and by depositing these Indian Reserves in London, Indian banking is retarded, and the prosperity of the country suffers. In his memorandum submitted to the Chamberlain Commission, Sir M. De P. Webb[2] says, "In connection with the general policy of holding the bulk of the Gold Standard Reserve in London, I submit that the Government have gone entirely beyond their province in undertaking to provide not only gold for export but gold ready delivered at a financial centre on the other side of the globe." And again, "To deposit the bulk of the gold in a centre where the banking community are already, on their own initiative,

1. K. T. Shah's *The Wealth and Taxable Capacity of India*, page 282.
2. Wadia and Joshi : *Money & Money Market in India*, page 250.

considering how they can strengthen their own admittedly slender and inadequate gold reserves, is to expose India to risks and dangers from which she has every right to expect complete protection." Profs. Wadia and Joshi state,[1] "The Government assumes the function of a banker, and wielding irresponsible power, can manipulate reserves on grounds not purely economic, and on considerations not entirely directed to the promotion of the trade and the industrial prosperity of the country."

In this manner, both by unproductive, exorbitant and wasteful expenditures, and by currency policy not calculated to further the interests of the people of the land, the disbursement of the Government have tended to impoverish the people. When we remember that such conditions have obtained generation after generation, is it difficult to understand the present poverty-stricken state of India?

---

1. Wadia and Joshi: *Money & Money Market in India*, page 250.

V

PUBLIC REVENUE

In a poor agricultural country like India, the bulk of the revenue has to be obtained from the masses and mostly through indirect taxation. Hence a great responsibility rests on the administration to see, that the articles of necessity to the poorer classes are not unduly heavily taxed, while as far as possible, the regressive tendency of the system should be alleviated by direct progressive and degressive taxation. Customs duty etc. should be so carefully scheduled as to be light on articles needed by the masses and heavier on those consumed by the comparatively well-off. While it is desirable to have a burden of the cost of Government distributed throughout the population, it is at the same time very unwise to bear too heavily on the poor. All available sources should be tapped before pressing on necessaries of life.

Cost of collection or the principle of efficiency has to be kept in view. Any great increase may indicate defects in the system—either in the administration or in principle.

In such of the Government activities as are of a commercial or of an industrial nature affecting the poorer strata, the principle of Fees and Deficit, rather than that of Profit, should be applied, bearing in mind the needs of the development of the country. This would apply especially to irrigation and to transportation rates, which affect the cost of production of the commodities produced by the poorer classes.

The prevalent ignorance in an illiterate country throws a further duty on the Government to check undesirable consumption by taxation without reference to the revenue produced.

In raising revenue, apart from the faculty of the people, the taxpayers' convenience of payment, both as regards time and method, has to be considered, as also the effect such payment will have on future production.

The system has to be so arranged as to produce a dependable stream of revenue to carry on the government, and at the same time not work any hardship on any of the producers.

The following figures for 1925-26 are constructed from the Statistical Abstract to show the net yield of each item of revenue after deducting the cost of collection, and cover both Central and Provincial Government revenues:

	Percentage of collection cost to gross yield		Net yield
Customs	1.7%	Rs.	46,96,18,017
Taxes on Income	3.6%		15,53,32,134
Salt	19.7%		5,07,90,619
Opium	50.8%		2,03,52,437
Land Revenue	11.6%		31,43,79,324
Excise on liquors, drugs, etc.			17,29,13,641
Stamps			13,28,52,205
Forests			2,60,31,029
Registration			78,14,679
Tributes			84,29,482
Scheduled Taxes			34,78,210

	Receipts	Expenses	
Railways	34,43,40,759	28,92,17,787	5,61,22,972
Irrigation	3,74,94,549	1,35,90,525	2,39,04,024
Post and Telegraph	86,35,220	50,69,134	35,66,085
Interests			6,56,02,939
Currency and Mint	4,63,89,101	70,11,413	3,93,78,688
Extra-ordinary	2,18,69,202	26,34,719	1,92,34,483
		Total revenues Rs.	1,56,88,00,968

CUSTOMS

It is rather difficult to trace the incidence of these duties owing to the classification used. But a careful scrutiny reveals the following as regards customs revenue:

	Lakhs of rupees
Export Duties	5,89
Excise on Petrol	77
Import Duties:	
on motor cars, cycles, etc.	3,32
on liquors & drugs	2,54
on machinery, rolling stock, etc.	1,24
on manufactured goods, textiles, cutlery, etc.	8,29
Total	2,205

Roughly we may take the above to represent the part of the revenue that falls on the better-off classes. To the net yield from Customs of 4,696 lakhs if we add 4% on 2,205 lakhs for expenses and refunds to the better-off classes we have 4,784 lakhs from this if we deduct their burden we have left (4,784 — 2,205) 2,579 lakhs which would represent the burden that falls on the poor. Government statisticts leave a great deal to be desired in furnishing the required information to enable us to allocate the tax burdens to the different strata of society, and it is very difficult to make comparisons over a period of years with any degree of accuracy. However, it is not difficult to discern a marked tendency to increase in all items without allowing for any variations in the value of the rupee.

When we remember that India is an agricultural country, we find that the receipts under customs are comparatively low. A larger proportion of the total revenue should be derived from this source. The 'Free Trade' policy forced on India is responsible for letting off this source of revenue so lightly. The British Board of Trade compiled a list of comparative foreign and colonial tariffs on British exports in 1904, giving the following[1] figures:

Russia	131	Rumania	14
Spain	76	Belgium	13
U. S. A.	73	Norway	12
Portugal	71	New Zealand	9
Austria Hungary	35	Japan	9
France	34	Turkey	8
Argentine Republic	28	Switzerland	7
Italy	27	Australia	6
Germany	25	South Africa	6
Sweden	23	China	5
Greece	19	Holland	3
Denmark	18	British India	3
Canada	17		

This discloses how little this source has been tapped, especially as the bulk of Indian imports are from Great

1. C. N. Vakil's *Financial Developments in Modern India*, page 442.

Britain, while the other countries and even the other members of the empire profit by a higher duty. Also in the export duties the convenience of the consumers in England receives the first consideration. Wheat, which is largely exported to Great Britain, if taxed, will be available to the Indian consumers at lower prices. As Prof. Marshall says: [1] "A protective tax in a country exporting raw produce and importing manufactured goods does not raise the cost of the goods to the consumers in that country by its full amount." Of course, it may affect the land revenue somewhat by a fall in cultivation, but as millions of the poor go with hardly a square meal a day, the restricted export and a fall in the prices may increase internal consumption, and in the absence of any definite data, it will not be possible to forecast whether the Government will gain or lose in the long run, but it is certain that the people of India will have more food grains available than at present. This may be one constructive way of meeting famines.

The benefit from lower prices, derived from the free trade policy, is in the interests of the class which uses imported fabrics etc., which class is generally composed of Europeans and well-to-do Indians. As this source of revenue is let off so lightly, the requisite revenue for the Government has to be raised in some other way, and this is done by heavier taxes on land, salt, etc., which taxes fall on the economic strata of society lower than the one which enjoys imported articles, who have no voice to complain.

Apart from low import duties, there are countervailing excise duties, making the tariff one of revenue rather than one of protection. Although the much criticized cotton duty was removed in 1926, it was not before it had practically wrecked at least one industry in which India had undoubtedly a comparative advantage. As Mr. Holland says: [2] "England's prosperity, and India's as a means to that, has in practice been the ruling consideration." And again:

1. Alfred Marshall's *Industry and Trade*, page 762.
2. W. E. S. Holland's *The Indian Outlook*, page 156.

[1]"But for a Government of India to have any other aim than India's welfare, or to be deflected by the competing interests of the ruling race, is to be guilty of treason against a nation committed to its trust." Alas! What beautiful sentiments, but Rev. Holland, being a missionary, evidently does not realize the hedonistic principles of life that govern the mundane affairs of everyday politics.

The result of the tariff policy pursued by the Government of India, combined with the discriminating railway rates described above, has been to reduce India to the position of 'a hewer of wood and a drawer of water' for Great Britain. How clearly we see illustrated, in the economic history of India, Prof. Marshall's statement:[2] "The more a country exported raw produce in return for manufactures, the less the benefit she got from the Law of Increasing Returns." Can India be anything but poor when such fiscal policies control her destiny?

Prof. Marshall writes:[3] "In all international trade policies her (Great Britain's) great Dominions are able to take full care of their own interests; but her Crown Colonies and India are not in equally strong positions; and therefore Britain is morally bound to attach to each of their interests at least as great a weight as if it were her own." And in a footnote he adds: "In particular no plea should be entertained for protective taxes on imports into Britain competitive with some of her own industries, however strong the national need for developing them may be, unless a similar principle is applied to selected Indian manufactures whose youthful strength is insufficient for competition on nearly even terms with rival imports from Britain and other Western countries." This is high idealism; to expect one to do unto another as one would like to be done by. It is difficult of attainment even in private life, then how much more remote is it in group life, and hardly to be looked for in politics in a nationalism-ridden world, where economic exploitation is the order of the day? It is amazing to find

1. W. E. S. Holland's *The Indian Outlook*, page 158.
2. Alfred Marshall's *Industry and Trade*, page 762.
3. *Ibid*, page 653.

the host of perfectly sane people who are led into believing that the Sermon on the Mount is the guiding principle of the Government of India. Mill, in a more practical way, observes that Government by a people is eventually for that people. In India, this has been proved true. Government by the British has turned out to be Government for the British. This is reflected in Mr. Holland's statement:[1] "So long as British policy in India is largely dictated by the requirements of the British trade and capital, Indians cannot feel that the political determination of their country's economic future can safely be left in foreign hands." And later on he observes:[2] "India's economic development must lack both health and vigour so long as she is politically dependent on an alien race." This same author quotes a Dundee jute merchant as having said to a Governor of Bengal not long ago:[3] "It is a grand country, it is an awful pity the native is in it." How very human even Britishers are! Free trade policy is all right among equally well developed peoples. It resolves itself into an exploitation of the less developed by the more developed in an unequal world, especially so if the latter control the fiscal policies of the former. Within definite limits, protection is helpful to develop nascent industries if the country has a comparative advantage in it.

Similarly 'Imperial Preference,' with all the other members of the Empire controlling their own destinies and India without fiscal autonomy, reduces itself into 'a Preference of Great Britain.'

INCOME TAX

In all taxation systems, income tax is gaining ground all over the world as the most satisfactory amongst taxes. While taxes of all kinds are pressing heavily on the poor in India, this tax is not yielding what it should. Some incomes are left immune from taxation. The Government of India pays interest on its debt in England, which country being outside its jurisdiction, no tax is deductable from

1. W. E. S. Holland's *The Indian Outlook*, page 162.
2. *Ibid*, page 166.
3. *Ibid*, page 61.

those payments. The law should be altered to enable India, like all other countries, to deduct its tax from interests paid to its foreign creditors. Messrs. Shah and Khambata compute such a procedure will bring into the treasury two crores[1] of rupees *per annum.*

Another source of income tax that escapes its due share of tax burden is the income of large landlords who merely pay the land revenue assessment, which works out as a proportional tax, and are exempt from progressive income tax as their income is considered 'agricultural income'. Here the principle of ability to pay should be applied, and all incomes, whether from land or industries, above a subsistence level, should be uniformly assessed, making the rates such as to bring about a degressive tax on incomes. Again the same authorities estimate the gain to the revenue from such a policy at ten crores[2] of rupees *per annum.*

If we look upon death duties as a 'Back Tax', here again there is a considerable source of revenue left untapped, in that the estates of foreign merchants, who make their enormous fortunes in India and then retire to Great Britain, completely escape taxation. This is especially a serious situation in that practically all Britishers are only birds of passage, and fail to contribute their proper share to the Government under whose shelter and benign care they amass their fortunes, leaving the burden to be borne by the toilers of the soil in greater measure. A satisfactory scheme should be worked out in conjunction with the Government of Great Britain by which such estates will render to India the things that are India's. At present, an estate pays the duties in Great Britain, and the British taxpayer gets the benefit of the revenue that rightfully belongs to India.

SALT

It is hardly necessary to dwell on the injustice of a tax on salt in a country like India. This tax has been opposed bitterly by all leaders in India. It is an unqualified

1. K. T. Shah and Khambata: *The Wealth and Taxable Capacity of India*, page 277.
2. *Ibid*, page 278.

evil bringing ruin to the nation, not only fiscally but also socially. W. S. Blunt bears the following testimony:[1] "It is only the very poor who are obliged to stint themselves in salt; but the very poor are, unfortunately, the rule in Southern India. In the Deccan, moreover, its pressure is galling because natural salt lies on the ground, and the people are therefore starved of it, as it were in sight of plenty. In several villages, which I passed, the ryots told me that they had been reduced to driving the cattle by night to the places where salt is found, that they may lick it by stealth; but the guards impound them if they are caught infringing the law, and latterly orders have been given that the police should collect in heaps and destroy all salt whatever found in its natural state above ground. In other parts I heard of a kind of leprosy attacking persons deprived of this necessary article of diet. The price of salt sold to the people by the Government is reckoned at from 1,200 to 2,000 per cent on its cost value." Even from the point of view of the principle of efficiency, it stands condemned as the cost of collection is about 20 per cent of the gross yield. Mr. Ramsay MacDonald says:[2] "Salt tax is exaction and oppression, and if the people understood it, it would only lead to discontent. It is a survival of the general exploitation of India's poverty by a profit making company." Even the pretence, that this tax is necessary to make the people realize the responsibility of the Government will not hold in India where there is so much ignorance and illiteracy that the masses do not even know or understand that there is a tax on salt, and even if they did, they have no voice to express themselves. This is an argument that can only be used in a democratic Government that is responsible to the people. So, even politically this tax is unsound.

LAND REVENUE

It is not within the scope of this essay to examine the vexatious and much debated proposition whether this source

1. W. S. Blunt's *India under Ripon*, page 243.
2. J. R. MacDonald's *The Government of India*, page 127.

is a tax or a rent. After arguing the *pros* and *cons* of the question in his monumental work, *The Land Systems of British India*, Baden-Powell declares,[1] "The land revenue cannot then be considered as a rent," and adds: "I should be inclined to regard the charges as more in the nature of a tax on agricultural income." Whatever it is, as John Briggs says[2] in his *Present Land Tax in India*, "we have but one alternative, and that is to acknowledge in the first place the fallacy of that doctrine which assumes a right to take the whole surplus profit from the landholder and to recognize the opposite maxim, that the more which is left in his hands, the greater will be his means to contribute to the national wealth and consequently to the public revenues." To argue that the ryot continues to pay revenue and still cultivates, and therefore, the revenue he pays should be differential rent, is to assume the existence of that myth — the Economic Man. This argument cannot be maintained when the only alternative the ryot has is starvation. If he had several options, and if he exercised it in favour of paying revenue and tilling the land, only then will this argument carry some weight, and not when this is but Hobson's choice. Those who know the people of India know that there is very little mobility in the population. The farmer is firmly attached to his locality, and taxation is not going to drive him away from the land of his forefathers. The resistance to change is great, and there is no other field of occupation into which he could retire, leaving him the only alternative of paying the tax and being content with one meal a day. Perhaps Mr. Yusuf Ali is right when he describes[3] this as a "demand levied by the Indian Government on land according to well-understood but ill-defined custom."

The method of assessment differs in detail in the various parts of the country, but as a rule the amount to be paid by the ryot annually is fixed in terms of money. It is estimated on the expected yield, and holds good for a

1. B. H. Baden-Powell's *The Land Systems of British India*, Vol. I, page 240.
2. Quoted by Prof. V. G. Kale: *Indian Economics*, page 807.
3. A. Yusuf Ali's *The Making of India*, page 238.

long period of years, about 30 years. It bears no relation to the actual production or price in any one year, so that in bad years the farmer is forced into the hands of the moneylenders in order to pay the tax which averages about[1] 50% of the estimated rental of the land. Although the British claim that they are only following the precedents set up by the Moghuls, they have forgotten that these excessive tax rates were prevalent at an unsettled stage of the country's history, as a war measure[2]. To perpetuate a temporary heavy tax is to kill all progress. Apart from this, the Moghuls had given the option of either paying in money or contributing a share of the yield in kind. This supplied the needed safety valve; and in addition to that, it was a paternalistic Government which relaxed under trying conditions, and if it did not, it was overthrown. The British Government, on the other hand, is a bureaucracy which functions with the precision of a machine and almost as relentlessly, as it has neither a heart nor a soul. As the payment in kind entailed loss due to accidental causes in realizing the value of the produce brought in, the British Government shirked this burden and made payment in money obligatory. To obtain the necessary funds, the ryot was obliged to shoulder the loss consequent on sale at a low price in an already overstocked market and often was forced to borrow. This method of payment leads to great hardship on the peasants, and to his chronic indebtedness to the usurer. There is no minimum of subsistence allowed for, and very often the tax falls below the efficiency line, and becomes cumulative in its poverty production. Ramsay MacDonald dealing with this matter confesses,[3] that "over-assessment and the rigidity of payment, therefore, have undoubtedly tended to impoverish the people, and a system of revenue collection, thoroughly sound in theory, and meeting the requirements of unassailable economic doctrine, has in practice become a grievous method of oppression and the subject of formidable attack."

1. R. C. Dutt's *India of the Victorian Age*, page 12.
2. Dr. Bala Krishna: *Indian Journal of Economcis*, Oct. 1927.
3. J. R. MacDonald's *The Government of India*, page 141.

Commenting on the chronic indebtedness of the ryot, Mr. W. S. Blunt says,[1] "I believe, it may be stated absolutely, that the whole of peasant indebtedness originally came from the necessity thus imposed of finding coin to pay the land tax." "This is the last worst evil which English administration has brought upon the Indian peasantry." "We have given the ryot security from death by violence, but we have probably increased his danger of death by starvation." Certain efforts, however inadequate, are being made to save the ryot from the clutches of the moneylender by the creation of co-operative banks, but the prevention lies in lifting the tax burden which is bearing him down. According to Prof. Radhakamal Mukerji,[2] "five men cannot pay a direct tax in money amounting to 40% of gross produce and the interest on old debts at 25% upon three acres of overcropped soil, without danger in a bad year of catastrophe."

EXCISE

This relates mostly to country liquors etc., the duty on imported spirits being included under 'customs duty'. India has all along been a dry country, but now there is a steadily growing tendency towards alcoholism, thanks to the policies followed by the Government in its eagerness to obtain revenue irrespective of humanitarian considerations. In the face of continued agitation by Indian leaders against this policy fiscal needs still outweigh social demands. Even where the Government makes a pretence of controlling consumption, loopholes are left by which the fall in the consumption of country liquors is made up by an increase in the consumption of imported liquor, as the following passage[3] culled from the Bombay Presidency Administration Report 1927-28 illustrates: "There has been, moreover, a considerable increase in the consumption of foreign spirit, beer and stout, and it is stated that beer is replacing country spirit to a considerable extent especially in large towns. From this foreign liquor the Government of Bombay derives but little revenue." (Such revenue from customs belongs to the

1. W. S. Blunt's *India under Ripon*, pp. 245-6.
2. Radhakamal Mukerji's *The Rural Economy of India*, page 204.
3. *Bombay Presidency Administration Report*, *Part 1*, page XVII.

Government of India.) A share of the blame for reduced efficiency and fall in production could easily be traced to this Government supported and encouraged inebriety.

FORESTS

The policies of Government as regards forests are formulated and carried out with a great deal of credit generally, yet in its enforcement we perceive the same harsh treatment of the poor and an utter lack of consideration for their needs. "The *modus operandi* seems to have been needlessly violent and most injurious to the people,"[1] says Blunt; also: "the effect, in any case, has been disastrous. The leaves of trees are largely used in India for manure and the supply is now cut off. The pasture has been reduced and the cattle are dying of hunger. Where wood has been free from time immemorial, so much a load now has to be paid." These inconveniences, however small they may appear to be, all gather force as they are accumulated and retard production to an amazing degree.

RAILWAYS

While we were dealing with expenditures we noted the effect discriminating rates had on the development of industries. Here it remains for us to consider the influence of railways on the production of the masses. When development of transportation keeps pace with the economic demands, railways do not kill the carrying trade of the poor. Indeed, in the U. S. A. the automobile trucks threaten the railroads themselves. But in India, where the carrying trade was not sufficient to absorb all these forms of transport, the railways have displaced the bullock cart, and the cart owner has been given no other means of utilizing his time and effort. India's economic order is very peculiarly dependent on the climatic conditions of the country. Owing to the monsoon the farmer can only work on the land during certain seasons, and at that time he uses his bullocks for ploughing, raising water etc., and when that season is over, he yokes his bullocks to the cart and earns a livelihood as a carrier. With the advent

1. W. S. Blunt's *India under Ripon*, pages 241-42.

of the railway the latter occupation has been taken away from him, and now for a large portion of the year both he and his bullocks produce nothing and are out of employment. It is not here argued that the railways are an evil in themselves, but only that nothing has been found to take the place displaced by their coming, and circumstances have forced on the farmer a period of leisure which he could ill afford. Hence production is low and the farmer is poorer.

The railways themselves are operated on the principle of Profits. No doubt the Government needs the money, but it should first prune all extravagance in salaries and establishments, and then choose such sources as will not affect the production of the people adversely.

IRRIGATION

This is one of the greatest, if not the greatest, need of India. Even if India had fertile soil in abundance and a sufficiency of employment for all, yet the farmer will face starvation if nature is not harnessed and made to yield her supply of water where and when needed. Although the monsoon is regular, taking the country as a whole, yet it is not dependable when we consider smaller tracts of the land. Hence from time immemorial irrigation has been one of the chief functions of Government. Private philanthropy sunk wells and built village tanks, while Governments constructed dams to harness the rivers and canals to distribute the much sought element. Under the British regime railways have been the favourites, and irrigation had to be content with occasional favours, with the result that over half[1] the irrigated area is dependent on private effort, and mostly individual effort at that. It is only since the beginning of this century that a definite policy is discernible as regards irrigation, but it is still circumscribed by financial exigencies, rather than being moulded by the claims of agriculture, i. e. it does not get the precedence its importance deserves over other forms of expenditures.

1. K. T. Shah's *Sixty Years of Indian Finance*, page 294.

INTEREST

An analysis of Interest received discloses the following sources of income:

In India :	
Loans to Corporations, States etc.	227
Railways: Loans & Provident Funds	42
Cultivators	31
Sundries	29
	329
In England	327
Lakhs of rupees	656

As usual with Government statements, further information as regards rates of interests etc. is lacking. Assuming that these items of interest arise from more or less uniform rate of interest, we can presume that practically half the available funds are invested in England, while Indian industries are being starved for lack of capital, and even the cultivator gets the benefit arising only from a meagre 5% of the available Indian funds in the hands of the Government. A few months ago that eminent engineer and financier, Sir M. Visvesvaraya, addressing a group of young men at a college in Poona, said,[1] "Several young men of this part of the country educated in foreign countries have attempted to start industries, but there have been pitiful cases of failure among them, mainly because the support of Government and of the organized money power of the country was lacking. Public opinion is unable to exert any influence in such cases and Government have not been known to take any interest." And Sir Daniel Hamilton of Calcutta, paints the following picture:[2] "We have given the people a railway system which removes the surplus crops, but we have not given them a banking system to bring back the price. The world takes the surplus crops, the sowkar and

1. Sir M. Visvesvaraya's *The Country's Immediate Needs, Mysore Economic Journal*, Vol. XIV, September, 1928, page 419.

2. Sir D. Hamilton's *India: Her Present and Future, Calcutta Review*, July 1916, page 295.

the trader take the money, and the devil takes the people." When the available resources of a country are being used outside its boundaries, can its inhabitants acquire wealth? Can they be anything but poor when interests other than their welfare occupy the mind of the Government?

VI

PUBLIC DEBTS

In private finance a person borrows to make both ends meet, if he has not the chance of increasing his income according to his needs; whereas the State has taxing power in order to raise revenues to meet its requirements. But in the course of a fiscal year an unforeseen contingency may arise, as in the case of a call to defend the country against foreign invasion. In such a predicament, the State borrows what amount it requires. Excepting where the credit of a country is very bad indeed, it is hardly ever necessary to definitely mortgage any particular asset. In some countries revenues from particular sources have had to be mortgaged as security. Again, in the case of capital expenditures, the State may deem it wise to spread the cost of the asset over a period during which the benefit from such asset accrues, or it may desire to tap idle capital at a low rate from persons who can well spare it; in such cases also the amount needed may be raised by a public loan and the loan may be redeemed during the life of the asset. In both instances—an emergency or a capital requirement—where borrowing is resorted to, it hardly needs to be mentioned, the purpose should always be in the interests of the country which will pay the charges. When the representatives of the people incur such debts they are termed 'National Debts', and when the Government is not a representative Government such debts are called 'Public Debts'.

In most countries up to a century or two ago public credit, as we know it today, was not in existence. At that time the government or states depended on accumulated hoards to tide over emergencies. The development of modern methods of finance, in commercial as well as in public matters, has led to an increase in debts.

In India, public debt was an unknown factor until the advent of the British rule. Prior to that time, if the rulers of the State incurred any debt, it was their own personal affair, and the debt had nothing to do with the people over whom they ruled. In the days of Clive, India was under the East India Company, which was only a commercial body with certain territorial privileges. The administration of the country was run on a profit-making basis, and there was a steady transfer of capital from India to England. There was no need for an Indian debt as the necessary funds were procurable under feudal conditions of pillage and plunder. At this period of history, England was in a very low financial state. According to Brooks Adam,[1] about 1750 "the English iron industry was in full decline because of the destruction of the forests for fuel. At that time four-fifths of the iron used in the kingdom came from Sweden", and prior to 1760 "the machinery used for spinning cotton in Lancashire was almost as simple as in India." Inventors there were many, but the necessary finances to put the inventions into practical use were lacking. The heart may conceive and the brain may devise, but if there were no hands to execute such conceptions on a commercial scale, all would be in vain. The opportunity to supply the needed capital to translate such ideas into actions presented itself after the Battle of Plassey. Macaulay describing the situation after Plassey says:[2] "The shower of wealth now fell copiously on the Company and its servants. A sum of eight hundred thousand pounds sterling, in coined silver, was sent down the river from Moorshidabad to Fort William. Calcutta, which a few months before had been desolate, was now more prosperous than ever. Trade revival and the signs of affluence appeared in every English house. As to Clive, there was no limit to his acquisition but his own moderation." 'The empire builder' Clive thus secured the right to loot India and secure finances for Europe. Three years later the flying shuttle made its appearance, and four

1. *Law of Civilization and Decay*, page 313.
2. *Essay on Lord Clive, Vol. III*, page 240.

years later the Hargreaves Spinning Jenny. In 1768, Watts brought out his steam engine. The years 1779 saw 'the Mule' invented by Crompton, and the power loom was patented in 1785. This was the birth of the industrial revolution of England and the industrial devolution of India. The capital needed to exploit inventions was thus supplied by direct and indirect plunder from India.

[1] "Possibly since the world began no investment has ever yielded the profit reaped from the Indian plunder, because for nearly 50 years Great Britain stood without a competitor." Burke says that in 1750 there were not even 12 'Banker shops', while in 1790 they were to be found in every market town. [2] "Thus, the arrival of Bengal silver not only increased the mass of money, but stimulated its movement for at once in 1759 the bank issued 10 and 15 pound notes, and in the country private firms poured forth a flood of paper." Probably between Plassey and Waterloo about 1000 million pounds[3] were transferred from Indian hoards to English banks. We can hardly realize the enormity of this sum when we allow for the purchasing power of money in those days. It is interesting to note that in 1815 the whole national debt of England was only 861 million pounds, which was considerably below the estimated loot from India in the previous 50 years.

Naturally, under these conditions, when the representatives of the British Crown, namely the East India Company, were able to send such enormous amounts to England, there was no question of any public debt in India. Apart from barefaced looting by 'empire builders', other indirect methods were resorted to in order to transfer Indian funds to England under a cloak of decency. The revenues of the East India Company were not all spent on the taxpayers. Out of the revenues Indian goods were bought and exported to Europe for sale, the taxpayer getting no return whatsoever on this transaction. The

1. Brooks Adams, *Law of Civilization and Decay*, page 317.

2. *Ibid*, page 319.

3. William Digby's '*Prosperous*' *British India*, page 33.

average revenue so used between 1793 and 1812 was over 13 million pounds per year.[1]

Having abandoned the method of honest looting and having found transference of goods inconvenient, the British financial genius soon found a way of holding a tribute on the Indian taxpayer in a more effective manner. This way was, not to take the money or goods from India, but to debit India with Britain's charges. The result is absolutely the same as the two former methods, that is, the wealth production in India is diverted to England without the producer in India getting any benefit in return, thus impoverishing our country and relieving the burden on the Exchequer of Great Britain. The bulk of what is known today as the 'public debt of India', is built up by such false debits.

India has not got a 'National Debt' as there is no national government. But according to the Statistical Abstract, India had a 'Public Debt' on 31st March 1926 of over one thousand crores made up as given below:

In India:

Loans	368.29	
Treasury Bills etc.	49.65	
		417.94
Provident Fund, P. O. Savings Bank etc.		94.55
In England: @ 1/4 to the Re.		513.29
		Rs. 1025.78 Crores

Leaving aside Bills and current liabilities the others are classified as:

'Productive'	737.18
'Unproductive'	221.88
	Rs. 959.06 Crores

And again the 'productive debts' are distributed as:

Railways	626.06
Irrigation	96.04
Post & Telegraph	13.00
Forests, Salt etc.	2.08
	Rs. 737.18 Crores

1. *Minutes of Evidence on the Affairs of the East India Company* 1813.

All that the above figures signify is that to that date the government expenditures exceeded the revenues by over one thousand crores. The further details are thoroughly unreliable and mainly fictitious, as no specific loans have been incurred for productive or unproductive purposes or for any particular asset. It is not possible to earmark any specific loan as being due to Railways, or Irrigation, etc. The classification and distribution are both arbitrary. Even the original ratio of 'productive' and 'unproductive' debts has been constantly altered by the government policy of writing off 'unproductive' debts from surpluses of revenue. This was only acute accounting device to throw dust into the eyes of the public, so that the taxpayer may imagine that the bulk of the debt is represented by assets. If one is to scrutinize these debts, the first requisite is to do away with this window dressing and remember that the total of 'Public Debt' merely represents the overspending of the government: or accumulated deficits met by borrowing. When once this is cleared then the scrutiny will naturally narrow itself into one of investigating what items led to such excessive spending. As we have already explained, such items can be one of two kinds:

1. Emergency expenditures,
2. Capital expenditures.

If these have been incurred on behalf of the people and for the benefit of India, surely such liabilities rest on our shoulders. But if we find that our accounts have been debited with items which are not a proper charge, then such items have to be disallowed. The amounts so disallowed may total up to a figure either equal to, less than, or more than, the present figure of public debt, according as to whether the debt is wholly due to such items, or whether part of such emergent or capital expenditures have been met out of revenues and not wholly out of borrowing, or whether the public debt has been written off from time to time from surplus revenues. As a matter of fact, in India, the last is the case. Large amounts of surplus revenues have been utilized to write off these debts, especially those called 'unproductive', so that, if a proper account is made of all financial transactions which are capable of being challenged, the aggregate of such items will exceed the present public debt figures of one thousand crores. Whatever may be the amounts, the only deduction possible is that such amounts should be taken out from Indian accounts and charged to the proper parties.

At the last Karachi Congress, a select Committee was appointed "to carry out a scrutiny into the financial transactions of the East India Company and the British Government in India and the so-called Public Debt of India, and to report on the obligations, which should, in future, be borne by India or England." It will be found from the report[1] of this committee, which is now published, that they have drawn attention to the following erroneous charges to India :

Year	Subject of claim	Amount in crores	
Prior to 1857	External wars of the company	35	
	Interest on company's capital	15.120	50.120
1857	Cost of the 'Mutiny'		40.000
1874	Interest on company's capital	10.080	
	Redemption of the capital stock of the East India Company	12.000	22.080
1857-1900	Cost of external wars	37.500	
1914-1920	European War : Gift	189.000	
	Cost	170.700	397.200
1857-1931	Miscellaneous charges	20.000	
	In respect of Burmah	82.000	102.000
1916-1921	Reverse Council losses		35.000
	Premium paid to Railway companies on acquisition by the State		50.000
1916-1921	Cost of strategic railways		33.000
		Crores	729.400

The above claims do not include anything in respect of a share of the Military expenditure which the committee

1. *A summary of that committee's report is given in* Appendix E.

suggest should be claimed as being properly debitable to the Imperial Exchequer. One member has added a [1]note to the report in which he calculates such amount to come to Rs. 540.13 crores. This is moderate as it is about one-fourth of the Military Expenditures, while Mr. Ramsay MacDonald himself is certain that at least half of the army in India is an Imperial Army, and suggests that its cost should be met from Imperial Funds.

Again, there is no refund of interest claimed; and another [2]note to the report works out that a refund of Rs. 536.02 crores, out of a total amount of Rs. 1,050 crores, be paid out. Thus the improper charges to India would amount to:

	Crores
As per above statement	729.4
Share of Annual Military Expenditure	540.13
Interest paid out wrongly	536.02
	Rs. 1,805.55

The Indian taxpayer is charged Rs. 1,805½ crores which ought to fall on the British Exchequer. Bulk of these expenditures are due to British Imperialistic Policies and consequent wars. It is not possible to go into details here; we can but refer the reader to the report of the Congress Committee. Annually we are paying in Interest alone about Rs. 50 crores on these wrong debits to us. J. Ramsay MacDonald says[3]: "India does not export tables in order to satisfy its needs by an equivalent import of chairs, India exports tables in order to pay debts." John Stuart Mill says: "A country which makes regular payments to foreign countries, besides losing what it pays, loses also something more by the less advantageous terms on which it is forced to exchange its production for foreign commodities." This becomes worse still when the creditor country controls the finances and the Currency and Exchange Policy of the debtor country and has the placing of orders of materials etc. This has been the lot of India. She has not been able to demand adequate return for her money; and

1. and 2. These Notes are reproduced in Appendix E.

3. J. R MacDonald's *The Government of India*, page 149.

by hanging these false chains round her neck, Britain hopes to retain this stranglehold on her for years to come. If India is to recover her bargaining power in international markets, she has to shake off these stupefying chains and claim what is her due.

In regard to Military expenditures which have been charged to India Mr. MacDonald writes, "Undoubtedly, India has not been dealt with fairly in this respect. It has had to bear the expense of operations that have been mainly Imperial." "[1]When we stationed troops in other parts of the Empire we did not charge them upon the Colonies, but in India we have the influence of the dead hand. When the Company ruled, it hired troops from Great Britain, and not only maintained them when in India, but paid the cost of their transport. When the Company surrendered to the Crown, the habit of 'lending' troops was kept up, as a fiction convenient to the Treasury of Great Britain. Owing to the report of the Financial Commission in 1900 the Home Government now pays £ 130,000 per annum, which is supposed to be about one-half of the cost of transport, and £ 100,000 is charged to the Home Treasury for half the Military costs of Aden. That is all. India pays the rest. Thus India is treated as an independent State, which, however, we rule and whose Military policy we control, while, it 'borrows' from us certain number of troops for which it pays; the arrangement is most unsatisfactory." Then he goes on to add about the external wars:[2] "The Commission which reported in 1900 put an end, it is to be hoped, to a still greater grievance. Frontier wars and wars of Annexation, like the Burmese wars, as well as the Abyssinian Expedition, were all paid for by the Indian taxpayer. Only £ 5,000,000 of the £ 21,000,000 which the Afghan War cost, was found by the Imperial Exchequer. These expeditions are in reality events in Imperial Policy and should not be an Indian charge at all. Mr. Gokhale once described the position

1. J. R. MacDonald's *Government of India*, page 154.
2. *Ibid.* page 155.

thus: "England has in the past borrowed troops from India for expeditions undertaken from considerations of Imperial Policy, such as the expeditions to China and Persia, the Abyssinian Expedition, and others, and on all these occasions all the ordinary expenses of these troops have been taken from India, England defraying the extraordinary expenses alone. On the other hand, when India had to borrow troops from England, as on the occasion of the Sind Campaign of 1846, the Punjab Campaign of 1849, and the Mutiny of 1857, every farthing of the expenses of these men, ordinary and extraordinary, including even the expenditure on their recruitment, was extorted from India." The Commission's Report met this particular grievance, but self-government would completely end unjust dealing and charge the Imperial Exchequer with expeditions that are Imperial.

"On the civil side, there are several payments objectionable to a degree which cannot be measured merely by the amount of the charges. The cost of the Secretary of State's establishment in London is charged to the Indian revenues. The Colonial Office is not so charged to the Colonies. Royal visits to India and the visits of the Secretaries of State are also paid for by the Indian taxpayer. These items, which now amount to about four hundred thousand pounds, are steadily growing. They are all Imperial costs and, in the main, are fixed apart from the Indian Government. Their appearance in the Indian Budget is mean and is altogether unworthy of us.

"One other item in Indian Expenditure calls for notice on account of its unfairness to India. For a long time, the value of the rupee was in relation to gold as one to ten, e. g. the rupee in Great Britain exchanged for 2 s. in 1873-4; it began to fall and lost 2½ d.; it went down slowly but steadily, every drop of a penny meaning the addition of a crore of rupees to Indian indebtedness which had to be met on a gold basis. In 1895 it had fallen to 1 s. 1d.; the mints were closed and the policy begun which created a token rupee, bearing the conventional value of 1 s. 4 d. Officers who had to send home money were badly hit; from 1893 additions were made to salaries of most Europeans, called "exchange compensations allowances", and in 1912, owing to the settlement of the value of the rupee, the Government issued a decision to add to European salaries amounts equal to these exchange allowances. This again is unfair to the Indian taxpayer. Certainly the officer ought not to suffer, but the fact that exchange considerations affect his real salary is not an Indian affair at all, but an Imperial one, and these extra emoluments should be found by the British Treasury.

"Indeed, the question is wider than this. When the Indian Exchanges were being so grievously disturbed, the disturbance was common to all 'silver' countries. But British policy in India was responsible for a good deal of the Indian unsettlement, and India's obligations to Great Britain seriously increased the difficulty.

"The controversy on the exchange is voluminous, complicated and obscure in some of its points, but since this country was responsible for the policy which brought the rupee problem to a critical head, it ought not to have left India to pay the whole expense of the depreciation, least of all that part involved in the payments made to the Government in London and its own servants in India."

It is suggested that as part of that 1800 crores has been paid off we should not raise any questions regarding that part. This is a queer argument put forward by want of clear thinking. If a merchant debits a customer with Rs. 1800 and the merchant has been taking interest on it before the customer enquired into the occasion for the debit and has also taken Rs. 800 on account of the principal, has the merchant any right to say to the customer, when he demands an account, "As I have taken Rs. 800 towards the principal we shall only have particulars for the balance and you have to forget all about the 800 rupees which has already been paid off"? If there is any part of the Indian debt that has been paid off, who paid it off? It is the Indian taxpayer, and if it is wrongly taken from him, he has to be compensated for.

According to the above account over Rs. 800 crores is due to India from Great Britain. Even if Great Britain takes over the whole of the 'Public Debt', the present bond-holders need not lose a penny if Great Britain possesses any sense of commercial morality. If they lose, they lose because of Great Britain repudiating her just debts. Will the country which laughed to scorn the Russians follow in their footsteps and hold its head up amongst honourable nations of the world?

VII

STERLING CREDITS

In the previous chapter we noticed the different devices used to secure at the cost of India the finances needed by Great Britain. This tradition was inaugurated by the Empire Builder Clive with his barefaced loot which was commendable at least for its avowed and undisguised nature. The methods that were adopted by his successors were in the order of increasing concealment of the real purpose of the transaction. The East India Company, which followed on the footsteps of Clive, adopted a more convenient but concealed way of transferring the wealth of India to Great Britain by utilizing Indian revenues for buying commodities for export to Great Britain for sale. This course was improved upon by the British Treasury which by a subtle system of accounting managed to debit to India all kinds of expenses and costs of Imperial Wars legitimately chargeable to Great Britain. The layman would find it almost impossible to find his way to facts through the maze of figures. During World War I a still better and simpler method was devised. By this large items of war expenses were wiped out against "Freewill gifts" made by the "Government of India" which was only a subordinate department of Whitehall. In this manner what was really a repudiation of debt was made to look respectable and seem honourable.

We have to look at World War II for the latest development in the scheme for the financing of Great Britain with funds from India. Under this method a semblance of honest contract is made by depositing an acknowledgement against materials taken out of the country without affording our country any facilities for benefitting by its credits. This method is simplicity itself. There is a flaw in the Reserve Bank Act. While providing for the backing of currency notes, bullion which possesses intrinsic value, and sterling securities, which represent merely the credit of

Great Britain, are both placed on the same level by the Act. This is contrary to sound financial principles. Advantage has been taken of this subtle provision to put into circulation unlimited quantities of notes. Paper acknowledgements, under the grandiose name of "Sterling Securities", to the tune of hundreds of crores are deposited with the Reserve Bank of India and currency notes to an equivalent amount are printed off. In this manner the notes in circulation which were about 200 crores in 1939 have been increased by about 1000 crores in the following five years while the gold backing remained the same throughout viz: 44 crores. Thus on the basis of gold the value of the rupee is now about seven pies.

With this easily manufactured purchasing power valuable commodities such as food grains, jute, tea etc. were secured at conveniently controlled rates and exported out of the country through the instrumentality of the specially formed agency of the government—The United Kingdom Commercial Corporation. By this device Great Britain obtained possession of commercial commodities in return for promissory notes and India was made to part with her production against frozen credits. Our circulation of note issue has been inflated to nearly six times its original volume without any compensating increase in the quantity of commodities either by imports from abroad or by accelerating internal production. This has resulted in unprecedented conditions of inflation in our country. Referring to this enormous stock of Sterling Securities thus built up to the credit of the Government of India the Chancellor of the Exchequer drew the attention of the House of Commons to the easement caused to British Finance by the generosity of the Government of India! Generosity indeed at the cost of the dumb starving millions.

THE ROLL OF THE U. K. C. C.

In regard to the part played by the United Kingdom Commercial Corporation in this high finance, Sir Francis Joseph, the President of this body, stated in London, "When the Corporation began to operate in India in June 1940, it was necessary to get a great variety of goods quickly to the near and Middle East . . . India was now one of the major supply bases of the United Nations. With the help of the Government of India the Corporation had lost no time in drawing on this source for supplies urgently required. Prompt shipment of Indian wheat had spared Persia the rigours of famine in the spring and early summer of 1941. Persia had received from India foodstuffs such as sugar, tea, manufactures such as cotton piece goods and raw materials. Shipments ranged in bulk from several thousand tons, lots of cement to small parcels of pharmaceuticals. Syria and Palestine were other Middle East countries which have drawn on India for supplies. Turkey received iron and steel, cotton yarn, hessian cloth, jute bags, ropes and hides. . . . It was clear that part of Russia's needs could be met from India. Orders were at once placed for a long list of commodities all for prompt delivery and in very large quantities. The list covered such articles as hessian gunny sacks, jute ropes, cotton canvas, hides, shellac, tea, groundnuts, tobacco and graphite. It is not possible to give details of actual tonnages, but the scope of business done in India for Russia was indicated by the fact that one recent order was for eleven million gunny bags."

This is robbing Peter to pay Paul. We may save Persia from famine, but India, which is already underfed and sparsely clothed is not the place from which to snatch away this food or all this valuble material in effect in return for Sterling Securities and that too at prices controlled by Government. India received no commodity in exchange which fact in itself would be sufficient cause for inflation as these exports are not products of excess output, but are taken mostly out of the normal stock of the country. In any case, half-starved and ill-clad India should be the last place to be asked to stint itself to supply rupee finance to Great Britain.

The paper currency of India has been increased to pay for Great Britain's war purchases and costs by setting aside the normal checks by ordinances of the Governor-General

INSECURITY OF STERLING PAPER

As we have already mentioned "Sterling Securities" represent merely the credit of Great Britain and are in effect purely promissory notes. A promissory note derives its value from the credit standing of the promissor which again is affected by the assets and liabilities of the debtor. The debtor — Great Britain in this case — has been spending at the average rate of about five thousand million pounds per year on the war and to meet this enormous outgoing she has been obliged to launch on a programme of disinvestment and has cashed in to the extent of thousands of crorers of her foreign securities. This indeed is an alarming state of falling credit. Promissory notes of such a debtor, when coupled with the prospect of these Sterling Securities being frozen for decades after the war, carry little value. If these credits are not encashable, as the financiers of Great Britain would have them, India cannot use them for obtaining goods from abroad excepting in accordance with the convenience and pleasure of Great Britain. In this manner, to accommodate Great Britain financially, India's political subjection has been exploited depriving her of her rightful dues.

STABILITY OF PURCHASING POWER

The need of our country for a stable currency is great. We have noticed that the quantity of currency notes in circulation is being increased without reference to our needs. This causes upheavals in the purchasing power of money. Unlike industrialized countries an agricultural country requires a medium of exchange with a solid backing to ensure stability of purchasing power, for, in industrialized countries the factor of time plays little part in the currency or the intermediate. A capitalist gets the sale proceeds of his goods and pays it into his bank immediately. A labourer gets his wages and exchanges that purchasing power for consumable articles within a week or a month before any change in the value of money can take place. On the other hand, in an agricultural country a farmer sells his produce after the harvest and, as no banking facilities are available to him in the village, he has to preserve his proceeds as best as he can till the next harvest. Therefore, it is essential for a farmer to have an intermediate with a steady intrinsic value which he can store away conveniently. Thus the hoarding habit of farmers is not an incorrigible perversity but is an unavoidable necessity arising out of the nature of their seasonal occupation. Hoarding can be countered only by an efficient organization of a chain of multiple co-operative societies which will take in the produce and market it and finance the farmers in the meanwhile. Until we have such facilities open to the rural population treasure troves supply a fundamental need and the yellow metal will have to be made available for the purpose. Decrying hoarding without understanding its place in the present economy only betrays ignorance or callousness.

Ours is an agricultural country where the intermediate has to serve a dual purpose—(a) as medium of exchange and (b) as a means of storing purchasing power. Often the latter function overshadows the former. Our masses do not invest to live on the unearned income. They are content to keep their capital intact. Hence this evaporation of the backing of currency notes and fall in their intrinsic value is of great consequence to our country. Even in highly industrialized Germany, under the stress of necessity people resorted to hoarding. When inflation was at its worst, the German people got rid of their money as fast as they could and obtaining whatever commodity they were able to get, hoarded their purchasing power for future use. Even farmers acquired machinery and instruments of production, which may never be used by themselves, as a means of preserving their purchasing power for future use. This function of our currency is frequently overlooked. To ensure this aspect it is essential to maintain the intrinsic value of our currency by an adequate backing in gold or make bullion available to the people against notes. Instead of this kind of a medium of exchange what is offered today is a fiduciary issue of notes with great instability of purchasing power.

CONCLUSION

Much has been said about India having benefitted through this war and having become a creditor of Great Britain instead of being as before a debtor. As long as she is deprived of her position in the world markets as an independent purchaser there is little consolation in piling up paper credits in London obtained through the suffering, nay starvation to death, of millions of villagers. The price that has been paid in actual commodities has been colossal as they have been taken at controlled rates, ignoring the needs of the producers themselves. Thus even in the process of credits accruing to our country we are in effect being impoverished—such is the irony of fate! We are creditors left to the tender mercies of our debtors.

VIII
SUMMARY

History teaches us that when a great empire disintegrates there is usually a scramble amongst the ambitious ones to seize what power they can. The British East India Company, which was a profit-making enterprise, availed itself of the opportunity and snatched the sceptre of the Emperor at Delhi. Perhaps owing to the prevailing unsettled conditions at the time, to the cost of wars when the Moghul Empire came tottering down, and to the tyranny of the last of the Great Moghuls, taxation was heavy in India and the economic state of the country was in a ferment. With true British loyalty to precedence the oppressive taxes were continued into peaceful times. With the added rigour of organization and strict administration these same taxes in the very same provinces brought in considerably more revenues than they did under the Moghuls. It was not a 'trusteeship' then, but a mere, honest, business proposition of exploitation. This idea is of much later growth, and came in as a rationalization to justify the British hold on India. In the early days of British domination, Empire builders, such as Clive and Warren Hastings, swept the country of all the wealth they could lay hands on. This provided the British with the millions that were necessary to capitalize the advantages of inventions of steam power etc., and in a large measure gave the lead to the 'Industrial Revolution' of Europe. What was the gain of Europe in general and of England in particular was India's loss, and started the downward journey in the economic history of this country. It was but to be expected that England should feather her nest, and she did it very well. The East India Company was purely a commercial concern in its make up, and it would be folly to look for any consideration for the development of India in its policies. Like all other private undertakings its outlook was circumscribed mainly by immediate gains rather than by a long-time view of affairs. India's interests, if they were recognized at all, were subordinated to England's bid for the economic supremacy of the world. India merely provided the stepping stone and the means of achieving her own ends. The speed on a downward journey is often accelerated beyond expectation by some added impetus. Whether the Britishers were conscious of the results they were bringing about or not, the stagnation in economic activity at the time of the fall of the Moghul Empire was followed by a rapid retrogression gathering momentum from the policies of the alien rulers.

Factorization was growing apace in England, and India was used as a plantation to feed these factories with requisite raw materials. England and India formed a vertical industrial unit controlled by financiers in England. The Indians' part in it "was not to reason why, theirs but to do and die". Such were the forces which formulated the tariff rates for India. Mr. MacDonald, while granting that the results of the policies of Government have proved to be inimical to the interests of India, pleads that that does not indicate that the Britisher was motivated wrongly: but attributes it to the fact that the Government[1] "happened to believe in principles of International Trade which coincided with Lancashire interests". This plea might find justification if the situation was the result of an error of judgment of one individual or of even a generation of administrators; but when we find it has been followed decade after decade by several generations, to grant Mr. MacDonald his contention would be tantamount to calling into question the intelligence of the best products of British universities from whom the Indian civilian is picked. The latter proposition — doubting the intelligence of the Indian civilian — is harder to accept than the former — that their motives were inimical to India's interest — which not only seems human — to consider the interests of one's own country first — but is a deduction from events spread over a century. When we remember that during all

1. J. R. MacDonald's *The Government of India*, pages 128-29.

that period the Indian leaders were constantly pointing out the evil effects the policy of Government was having, it is too great a draft on our credulity to ask us to believe that this destructive policy was pursued quite unconsciously by well-meaning but ignorant civilians.

Railways were developed to carry out the scheme, and discriminating rates supplemented the tariff, and all worked harmoniously but for the discordant notes struck by the 'disgruntled agitators' in India and by their 'ill-advised' sponsors in England. In the main, the exploitation policy of the East India Company was continued when the British Crown assumed responsibility for India, although it was no longer a barefaced commercial concern but was heralded by high-sounding trumpets of Divine Ordinance, but those 'natives' who had not the gift of musical appreciation only heard the roar of hungry imperialism.

With such political and historical background it is easy to understand the fiscal policies followed. India was made to pay as much as possible in return for as little as was necessary to keep up appearances of exchange. Indeed, as someone has put it, "India was twice blessed — blessed in the trade profits it gives to Great Britain, and blessed also in the protection it takes at high market values." The general fiscal set up has not been one calculated to increase the productivity of the people of the land. Very large amounts have been sunk in capital expenditure which had very little value in aiding the production of the masses, while other forms of developmental expenditures which were essential to promote the welfare of the country were stinted. Nation-building expenses have received hardly any attention, while Empire-building schemes have sucked dry all available resources. In the words of Mr. MacDonald, "We[1] spend far too much of the income of India on Imperial purposes and far too little on Indian development." The clamours of the ruling class have made inaudible the sighs of the suffering masses.

1. J. R. MacDonald's *The Awakening of India*, page 148.

The revenues are collected in India but a large part is spent in England. "When[1] all is said and done, and a balance of advantage and disadvantage struck, I think there can be no doubt, that India suffers greatly because so much of its created wealth is spent and fructifies outside itself," says MacDonald.

While the revenues are obtained from the poor, they are utilized in keeping up the prestige of the foreign ruler. Again to cite the same Labour leader[2] : "Indian revenues have always been taken far too much from the poor, and the rich have got off far too lightly." Sir A. Collin stated[3] : "The immunity of the middle and upper classes from their due share of the public burdens is . . . a grievous blot on our Indian administration which urgently calls for removal." The poor man's rupee, saved by giving up nourishing food, helps to maintain the luxury of the rich: thus resulting in a loss of 'marginal utility' in the tax funds and so of the National Income. Sir Wm. Hunter, dealing with land revenue, admits[4]: "The Government assessment does not leave enough food to the cultivator to support himself and family throughout the year."

It may be asked: Why should the Government tax the poor heavily and let the well-to-do classes pay comparatively little? It has been suggested that it is a discrimination in favour of the Britishers, as all Britishers in India, practically without exception, fall into such a class. There is another answer to that question—a much sounder one—and under the conditions obtaining in India it would be surprising if things were differently ordered. That reason is a political one. The British Government in India is an alien Government without any roots by which it could draw the sap from the people of the land. It needs the sympathy and support of at least some of the people. That section of the populace, whose loyalty is worth

1. J. R. MacDonald's *The Government of India*, page 149.

2. *Ibid.* page 128.

3. Quoted by V. G. Kale: *Indian Economics*, page 951.

4. Quoted by Lajpat Rai: *Unhappy India*, page 356.

courting and whose power, and influence count most, especially in a bureaucracy, is that educated upper layer which forms the economic aristocracy, and it is this group which is placated by the tax system. It also happens that the interests of this class are closely intertwined with the interests of Britishers; and their protests against any measures that may affect them adversely are far more effective in Government circles.

The expenses of an alien Government are likewise increased by circumstances which do not exist under a national Government. For instance, an alien Government has to depend on a mercenary standing army which must be maintained during peace and war. Only a national Government can keep expenditure down by supporting a comparatively small regular force and depending on the national reserves for emergencies.

The argument often advanced in an attempt to justify the railway policy, namely the mitigation of the horrors of famines, is like justifying the maintenance of an enormous navy, as it is capable of rendering useful rescue service in case of a gale or a storm; and it is no more logical when methods of preventing famines are ignored, private tanks and wells are closed, and irrigated water is supplied at monopoly prices and not infrequently, owing to a lack of scientific research facilities, such high priced water contains ingredients injurious to the crops. Even as a means of transport Sir. A. Cotton said[1]: "My great point is, what India wants is water carriage; that railways have completely failed, they cannot carry at the price required . . . Steam boat canals would not have cost one-eighth that of the railways; they would carry any quantities at nominal prices and at any speed."

Rushbrook Williams put his finger on the spot when he said[2]: "The real truth is that the undeniable poverty of India arises principally from the fact that the country is not organized for the production of wealth." The

1. Quoted by K. T. Shah: *Trade, Tariffs and Transport*, page 409.
2. Rushbrook Williams ,*India in 1923-24*, page 194.

following generalization[1] of J. A. Hobson supplies us with a reason why India is not so organized: "The civilized western world is coming more consciously to mould its practical policy, political and economic, and its sentiments and theories, upon a white exploitation of the lower and backward peoples. Imperialism is displacing, or at present is crossing, class supremacy, and is evolving an intellectualism and morals accommodated to the needs of this new social cleavage. It is moving towards a not distant epoch in which western white nations may, as regards the means of their livelihood, be mainly dependent upon the labour of regimented lower peoples in various distant portions of the globe, all or most members of the dominant people enjoying a life of comparative pleasure and leisure and a collective sense of personal superiority as the rulers of the earth." We find this idea expressed by Dr. Rutherford when he stigmatizes the British rule as is found in India as[2] "the lowest and most immoral system of Government in the world—the exploitation of one nation by another." He further traces the chief causes of India's poverty to the policies of the Government both as regards revenues and expenditures, and attributes them in particular to "neglect[3] of education of the masses, neglect of sanitation and medical services in the villages, neglect to keep up order; neglect of the housing of the poor, neglect to protect the peasant from the moneylenders, neglect to provide agricultural banks; comparative neglect to improve and develop agriculture; neglect to foster Indian industries; neglect to prevent British profiteers from capturing tramways, electric lighting and other public services; and neglect to prevent the manipulation of the currency in the interests of London."

Granting that protective tariff might not have prevented the old cottage industries and handicrafts from dying out, it would have promoted machine production and given

1. J. A. Hobson's *Work and Wealth*, page 156.

2. V. H. Rutherford's *Modern India*, page 77.

3. *Ibid.* page 161.

direction to newly forming industries which would have drawn the excess population from the farms to the cities, and thus increased agricultural production relative to the labour employed. Increased productivity with the co-operation of the producers to avoid the evils of capitalism would have brought relief to the poverty of the masses. "If[1] manufactures are crippled, agriculture overtaxed, and a third of the revenues remitted out of the country, any nation on earth would suffer from permanent poverty and recurring famines. Economic laws are the same in Asia as in Europe. If India is poor today, it is through the operation of economic causes. If India were prosperous under these circumstances it would be a miracle." The wonder is that India has been able to exist at all, and the economic miracle is that during the past decades India has been turning stones into bread. Any other nation under similar circumstances would have given up the ghost in desperation long ago. Ramsay MacDonald himself confesses[2]: "On the whole, I think, two charges can be substantiated against us: our Government is extravagant, and we have behaved meanly to India." If the nature of the Governmental expenditures were such as to increase the productivity of the people, it also increases their faculty; but on the other hand, if it were such as to reduce productivity, it impoverishes the people. If a large part of their production is sent out of the country in return for little in exchange, then to that extent there is less of the national income to be distributed. The *per capita* income was computed under Government direction as follows, on a similar basis each time:

By Baring and Barbour	1881	Rs. 27	per annum
For Lord Curzon	1901	Rs. 30	" "
By Prof. Shah	1921	Rs. 74	" "

On the face of it, it looks like progress; but money values have no meaning unless reduced to a common denominator in terms of purchasing power. When we reduce these according to the price index for the respective years, of

1. R. C. Dutt's *Economic History of India*, XVI.
2. J. R. MacDonald's *The Awakening of India*, page 148.
3. C. N. Vakil and Muranjan: *Currency and Prices in India*, page 309.

100, 120, and 378, we get the incomes for the three years respectively as Rs. 27, Rs. 20.37, and 19.6, a steady fall. Hyndman knows what he is talking about when he says:[1] "I can only repeat that the people of India are growing poorer and poorer; that taxation is not merely actually but relatively far heavier; that each successive scarcity widens the area of impoverishment and renders famines more frequent; that most of the trade is but an index to the poverty and crushing overtaxation of the people; that a highly organized foreign rule constitutes by itself a most terrible drain upon the country; and that all the railways and irrigation works on the planet if concentrated in India at the cost of the peasantry would but serve to hasten the inevitable catastrophe."

"Under a democratic and a representative Government, a steady growth in Government expenditures is generally regarded as an index of progress. But in India, when such growth is due to officials voting themselves higher salaries and allowances under the plea of rising prices, it is doubly harmful. The unproductive expenditures are increased without any advantage or return to the taxpayer, while his own income is reduced, so that a greater loss is incurred in the marginal utility of the national rupee. According to Sir Wm. Hunter: "It[2] profits little that we have put an end to invasion from without, established order and security in place of anarchy and rapine within, covered the land with schools and court houses, with roads, railways, and canals, and given a vast impulse to population and trade —all this profits little, if the people have not enough to eat, and if the country cannot support the cost of our rule."

Apart from these economic losses there is a further loss due to a lack of a full return for value. One of the greatest benefits that a nation reaps from its expenditures is the immeasurable advantage it derives from the accumulation of experience and wisdom by its administrators

1. H. M. Hyndman's *Bankruptcy of India*, page 74.

2. Sir Wm. Hunter's *India of the Queen*, page 134.

who, after their period of active public life, retire into the councils of the nation to aid and guide the next generation. The British civilian gains experience and the Indian taxpayer pays for it, but when mature, the civilian retires to Great Britain and India loses the advantage of the wisdom it has paid for, and that loss again is Britain's gain. Who can say how much Britain owes her present leadership in the political world to the wider range of viewpoint provided by her sons who were trained in India?

IX

CONCLUSION

After considering the ways and means of alleviating the poverty of the masses, W. S. Blunt suggests:[1] "I do not believe in legislative remedies for the starvation of the ryot or in the possibility of relieving his position except at the sacrifice of interests too strongly represented both in Calcutta and in London to be assailed with any chance of success. Finance, not legislature, is the cause of all the evil; and until that is put upon a sound footing, the rest is of no real value." We have to cease using the poor man's rupee and replace it by revenues from untapped, richer sources, and regulate equitably India's financial relations to the Empire. "If the empire would readjust the burdens which it imposes upon Indian Finance and if that were done and nothing more, the Indian Government could inaugurate great reforms which would increase Indian wealth," says[2] MacDonald.

As long as human nature is what it is, India's finances cannot be moulded to fit into India's needs, until the powers that be are goaded on by motives which are identical with India's interests. Taxation has to be such as will increase production and encourage activity. When taxation nurtures infant industries; when the revenues are drawn without injuring the sources; when the starving masses are not called upon to support an extravagant and luxurious administration; when those who make their fortunes under the hospitality of India are made to assume their due share of the burden of administration; when India's revenues are spent in such ways as to bring full returns to the people; when Government undertakings needed by the poor are operated on the principle of service, and the channels chosen do not run counter to those of national interests; when the choice of alternatives is determined by the needs of India; then and then only can India be expected to progress economically, and this cannot be until India wins fiscal autonomy.

1. W. S. Blunt's *India under Ripon*, page 247.
2. J. R. MacDonald's *The Government of India*, page 158

APPENDIX A

POPULATION

Census 1921: British Territory including Burma and Indian States

I. DISTRIBUTION OF POPULATION: RURAL AND URBAN

Class	No. of Villages or Towns	Per cent of Population	Population
Villages under 500	517,036	30.10	
500-2,000	152,259	43.05	
2,000-5,000	15,965	14.13	
Total Rural		87.28%	278,373,604
Towns 5,000-20,000	2,388	6.09	
20,000-100,000	253	2.97	
100,000 and over	34	2.53	
Total Urban		11.59%	37,602,286
Unclassified	46	1.13%	2,966,590
Total		100	318,942,480

II. DISTRIBUTION OF POPULATION ACCORDING TO OCCUPATION:

Production of Raw Materials	73.15%
Preparation and Supply of Material Substances:	
Industry, Transport, Trade, etc.	17.59
Public Forces & Administration	1.53
Professions	1.59
Miscellaneous	6.14
	100.00

III. Distribution of a Cross-section of the Population of 10,000 persons according to Religion, Sex & Literacy

Religion	Number Per 10,000 of Population	Literate Males	Per cent of Males	Literate Females	Per cent of Females	Literate Total	Illiterate Males	Per cent of Males	Illiterate Females	Per cent of Females	Illiterate Total	Remarks
Hindu	6,856	404	11.53	46	1.38	450	3,102	88.47	3,304	98.62	6,406	
Mahomedan	2,174	92	8.1	8	0.73	100	1,047	91.9	1,027	99.27	2,074	Mostly in Bengal, the Punjab the U. P. & Bihar & Orissa
Buddhist	366	84	48.44	12	6.19	96	89	51.56	181	93.81	270	Of the total, Burma contains 11,201,943 India 369,325
Animistic	309	2	1.4	...	0.12	2	153	98.6	154	99.88	307	Mostly in Bihar, Orissa, Central Pr., Berar, and Assam
Christian Europeans etc. 5.6 Anglo Indians 3.7 Indians 141.7	151	24	30.9	13	18.04	37	54	69.1	60	81.96	114	Mostly in Madras
Sikh	102	5	9.39	1	1.4	6	53	90.61	43	98.6	96	Mostly in the Punjab
Jain	37	10	51.34	1	7.6	11	9	48.66	17	92.4	26	Mostly in Bombay, the United Provinces & Central Provinces
Parsi	3	1.3	78.75	1	66.91	2.3	0.3	21.25	0.4	33.09	0.7	Mostly in Bombay
Jews and others	2	0.65	50	0.2	24	0.85	165	50	0.5	76	1.1	Mostly in Bombay, Bengal, Burma & Madras
Total	10,000	623		82		705	4,508		4,787		9,295	

IV. DENSITY AND GROWTH OF POPULATION IN BRITISH INDIA ALONE

As Government apologists constantly attribute the poverty of India to the rapid increase in population, the following table is prepared to supplement what has been stated on this subject in Chapter III. Absolute numbers at the end of each decade cannot be compared in India as the area of 'British India' has been constantly added to from time to time, and hence the population per square mile has been taken as the basis of comparison to allow for territorial increases. France has always been regarded as having an almost stationary population and England is considered a prosperous country, and so a helpful comparison with these countries is instituted.

Census Year	Population Per Square Mile India	France	England & Wales	With 1871 as base year India	France	England & Wales
1871	215	174	389	100	100	100
1881	227	182	445	105.5	104.6	114.4
1891	229	185	497	106.5	106.3	128
1901	210	188	558	97.6	108	143.4
1911	223	189	618	103.6	108.6	158.8
1921	226	184	649	105.1	105.7	166.8

Summary	India	France	England & Wales
Increase during the half century	5.1	5.7	66.8
Average increase per decade	1.0%	1.15%	13.3%

The normal increase should be about 10% per decade.

APPENDIX B

AGRICULTURAL STATISTICS FOR 1927-28

Food grains	Lakhs of Acres		Units	Yield Lakhs of units.
Rice	766		Tons	273
Wheat	246		„	63
Barley	68		„	21
Jowar	212		„	50
Bajra	141		„	24
Ragi	38			
Maize	59		„	23
Gram	140		„	32
Others	296			
		1,966		
Vegetables, Fruits & Spices		78		
Sugar	30		„	31
Coffee	1		lbs.	191
Tea	7		„	3,612
		38		
Oil seeds:				
Linseed	22		Tons	3
Sesamum	35		„	4
Rape & Mustard	33		„	8
Groundnut	47		„	25
Cocoanut	6			
Caster	6			
Others	12			
		161		
Cotton	148		400 Bales	101
Jute	33			
Other fibres	7			
Indigo & Opium	1			
Tobacco	11		Tons	6
Fodder	92			
		292		
		2,535		

APPENDIX C

TRADE STATISTICS, 1927-28

I. EXPORTS

Articles	Value in Lakhs of Rs.	Unit	Quantity
Animals	47	No.	570,530
Apparel	24		
Bran and Pollards	133	tons	270,875
Bristles & Brush Fibre	46	cwts.	160,950
Candles	12	lbs.	4,397,533
Coal & Coke	77	tons	634,507
Coffee	232	cwts.	276,668
Coir & Products	114	tons	33,587
Cotton: Raw	4,801	tons	482,336
Twist & Yarn	188	lbs.	24,696,890
Manufactures	679	yds.	168,623,708
Drugs & Medicines	35		
Dyes etc.	161	cwts.	2,143,471
Fish	87		
Fruits & Vegetables	106		
Grains and Pulse:			
Barley	85	tons	71,628
Beans	39	,,	41,977
Gram	28	,,	17,567
Jowar	35	,,	21,115
Lentils	29	,,	16,538
Maize	10	,,	9,496
Pulse	92	,,	57,252
Rice	3,401	,,	2,186,760
Wheat	441	,,	299,733
Wheat flour	130	,,	60,424
Others	3	,,	1,581
Gums & Resins	20	cwts.	66,636
Hemp: Raw	81	,,	484,146
Hides & Skins:			
Raw	881	tons	64,381
Tanned	907	,,	23,256
Horn	9	cwts.	43,110

Jute: Raw	3,066	tons	891,907
Manufactured	5,356	No. Bags	463,139,689
		cloth: yds.	1,552,751,590
Lac	699	cwts.	543,584
Manures: Bone	128	tons	120,312
Metals	897	,, Manganese ore	703,949
		others	673,729
Mica	93	cwts.	82,511
Oilcake	314	tons	275,595
Oils	71	gal.	1,458,212
Opium	199	cwts.	6,208
Paraffin Wax	242	tons	51,132
Provisions	61		
Rubber: Raw	257	lbs.	25,403,266
Saltpetre	12	cwts.	99,063
Seeds	2,670	tons	1,209,973
Silk: Raw	36	lbs.	1,332,519
Manufactures	6	yds.	881,154
Spices	240	cwts.	437,551
Sugar	8	tons	2,891
Tea	3,248	lbs.	361,614,124
Tea waste	4	,,	4,114,638
Tobacco	106	,,	29,246,489
Wood	166	Cub. tons	50,624
Wool: Raw	436	lbs.	50,165,892
Manufactures	97		
All other articles	570		
Total Rs.	31,915 lakhs		

II. IMPORTS

Articles	Value in Lakhs of Rs.	Unit	Quantity
Apparel	164		
Arms, ammunition etc.	71		
Belting for machinery	87		
Books	62		
Boots & shoes	67	pairs	2,772,964
Building materials	129		
Buttons	32		
Carriages	17		

Chemicals	265			
China clay	19		cwts.	533,795
Clocks & Watches	27		No.	630,246
Coal & coke	63		tons	273,818
Cotton: Raw	674		,,	66,062
Twist & Yarn	679		lbs.	52,344,534
Manufactures	5,836	Piecegoods	yds.	2,026,520,680
		Rope thread	lbs	4,859,997
		Blankets	,,	5,229,166
		Shawls	No.	8,310,447
Cutlery	39			
Cycles	118		,,	138,783
Drugs & medicines	198			
Dyeing etc.	265			
Fish	37			
Flax manufactures	37	Piecegoods	yds.	2,243,280
		Thread etc.	lbs.	659,980
Fruits & Vegetables	202			
Furniture	31			
Glassware	248	sheets & plate	sq. ft.	23,425,399
Grain, pulse & flour	231		tons	160,897
Gums & Resins	40		cwts.	189,118
Haberdashery	127			
Hardware	524			
Hides & Skins	35		tons	2,189
Horses	37		No.	4,001
Instruments etc.	447			
Ivory Manufactures	21		lbs.	276,562
Jewellery	152			
Jute Manufactures	24	Bags	No.	6,131,156
		Canvas	yds.	2,85,022
Leather ,,	57			
Liquors	367		Galls.	7,118,458
Machinery	1,594			
Matches	39			
Metals : Iron and Steel	2,144		tons	1,197,261
: Brass etc.	695		cwts.	2,588,196
Motor cars etc.	617		No.	25,950
Oil	1,108		Galls.	234,673,422

Paints etc.	155			
Paper, Paste board etc.	341	Materials	cwts.	399,350
Porcelain	80			
Provisions	641			
Railway Plant etc.	477			
Rubber goods	271			
Salt	175		tons	596,250
Seeds	18		cwts.	85,980
Ships	17			
Silk : Raw	145		lbs.	2,356,225
: Manufacture	360	Piecegoods	yds.	23,740,686
		Yarn	lbs.	1,440,683
Soap	161		cwts.	422,489
Spices	258		,,	1,118,734
Stationery	92			
Sugar	1,491		tons	822,902
Tallow	26		cwts.	93,514
Tea	69		lbs.	7,993,933
Tea chests	72			
Tobacco	291		lbs.	9,928,045
Toilet Requisites	62			
Toys & games	64			
Umbrellas etc.	62		No.	294,036
Wood & Timber	81	Timber cubic	tons	24,749
Wool : Raw	45		lbs.	5,781,996
		Piecegoods	yds.	18,776,855
: Goods	492	Shawls	No.	1,088,939
		carpets	lbs.	4,962,918
Others	1,413			
	24,985			

III. RE-EXPORTS (IMPORTS INTO INDIA AGAIN SHIPPED TO OTHER COUNTRIES)

Articles	Value in Lakhs of Rs.	Unit	Quantity
Apparel	13		
Cotton : Goods	121	yds.	33,791,217
: Yarn and Twist	15	lbs.	1,383,564
Fruits and Vegetables	20		
Gums and Resins	25	cwts.	60,041
Hardware	26		

Metals	26	tons	36,808
Provisions	3	cwts.	4,858
Spices	3	cwts.	7,846
Sugar	55	tons	19,812
Wool : Raw	89	lbs.	15,699,592
Others	558		
	954		

IV. BALANCE OF TRADE (*in Lakhs*)

Exports of Indian Merchandise		31,915
Less Imports of Foreign Merchandise	2,46,73	
Less Re-exports	954	23,719
Merchandise Balance in favour of India		81,96
Less Imports of gold, silver and currency notes		32,19
Net Trade Balance in favour of India		Rs. 49,77 lakhs

Note : Imports do not include railway materials imported by State Railways.

Part of the Balance was taken up by the British Government as follows :

Council Bills etc. to the United Kingdom	37,77
Interest Drafts on Government Securities	35
	Rs. 38,12 lakhs

V. TRADE WITH PRINCIPAL FOREIGN COUNTRIES

Countries	Exports in lakhs of Rs.	Imports in lakhs of Rs.
United Kingdom	78,91	1,19,27
U. S. A.	35,90	20,44
Germany	30,68	15,35
Japan	29,00	17,90
France	15,77	4,31
Ceylon	15,18	1,91
Italy	12,68	6,78
Belgium	10,85	7,49
S. America	10,67	8,33
	239,64	201,78
Others	79,51	48,07
	Rs. 3,19,15 lakhs	Rs. 2,49,85 lakhs,

APPENDIX D

ACCOUNTS 1927/28

One lakh = 100,000. 1 Re. = 1 sh. 6 d. = 36 cents (U. S. A.)

I. NET PUBLIC EXPENDITURES

Debt Services	18,49,49,736	13.3%
Military	54,79,45,581	39.4%
Civil Administration	58,30,91,611	41.9%
Miscellaneous	7,55,07,986	5.4%
	Rs. 139,14,94,913	100.00

Details of Civil Administration

	In Lakhs	Per cent
General administration	12,90	9.27
Audit	88	0.63
Justice	4,76	3.42
Jails	2,11	1.52
Police	11,80	8.48
Ports	24	0.17
Ecclesiastical	32	0.23
Political	1,58	1.14
Frontier Watch and Ward	2,50	1.80
Scientific	99	0.72
Education	11,88	8.54
Medical	3,53	2.54
Public Health	1,72	1.23
Agriculture	2,09	1.50
Industries	67	0.48
Aviation and Miscellaneous	30	0.21
Indian Stores Dept.	3	0.02
	58,30	41.90

II. NET REVENUE

	Collection cost to gross yield	Net yield
Customs	1.8%	47,36,60,338
Taxes on Income	4.3%	14,77,07,867
Salt	19.2%	5,36,66,898
Opium	22%	3,07,51,429

Land Revenue	11.9%		31,43,90,345
Excise on Liquors & Drugs			17,59,39,308
Stamps			13,28,24,933
Forest			2,69,08,190
Registration			75,86,616
Tributes			83,97,285
Scheduled			40,31,275
			1,37,58,64,484
	Receipts	Expenses	
Railways	38,72,28,944	32,40,35,381	6,31,93,563
Irrigation	2,83,99,739	1,33,90,700	1,50,09,039
Interest			5,97,67,686
Currency & Mint	2,77,46,116	70,11,413	2,07,34,703
Extraordinary	3,61,98,543	44,85,916	3,17,12,627
			1,56,62,82,102
less Post & Telegraphs	31,45,661	60,45,689	29,00,028
			Rs. 1,56,33,82,074

III. PUBLIC DEBT

In India			
Loans	3,72.24		
Treasury Bills etc.	39.53	411.77	
Provident Fund, P. O. Savings Bank etc.		119.19	
In England (@ 1/4 to the Re.)		516.60	
	Total Rs.	1047.56	Crores
'Productive' Debts		805.06	
'Unproductive' ,,		95.18	
	Rs.	900.23	Crores

Details of 'Productive' Debts

			In lakhs
Railways		39,712 miles	6,68,74
Irrigation	Main Canals	22,402 ,,	1,11,44
	Distribution	44,587 ,,	
Post & Telegraphs			14,66
Forest		11,03,579 Sq. Miles	1,47
Salt			86
Vizagapatam Harbour			1,26

Hydro-Electric Scheme	70
Bombay Development Scheme	4,16
Government Commercial Undertakings	1,77
Lakhs Rs.	8,05,06

IV. CUSTOMS REVENUE—DETAILS

Sea Customs—Imports

	In Thousands of Rs.
Arms, Ammunition and Military Stores	7,31
Coal, Coke and Patent fuel	1,60
Tin, block	8,20
Liquors	2,55,93
Matches etc.	53,72
Opium	3
Mineral Oils	1,78,92
Sugar	6,51,19
Tobacco	2,17,13
Artificial Silk Yarn and Thread	7,91
Cotton : Yarn and Thread	41,45
: Piecegoods	6,25,17
Silk Mixtures	7,26
Portland Cement	9,96
Printers' Ink	37
Motor Cars and Cycles	89,58
Duty at 2½%	
Machinery	21,90
Locomotive Engines and Tenders	68
Other Articles	53
Duty at 10%	
Metals—Iron and Steel	51,09
Railway Plant and Rolling Stock	28,94
Other Articles	1,07
Duty at 15%	
Articles of Food and Drink	1,82,09
Raw Materials	78,85
Cutlery, Hardware etc.	2,19,28
Yarn and Textile Fabrics (other than Cotton or Silk)	1,82,88

Pneumatic Rubber Tyres and Tubes		29,60
Other articles and Miscellaneous		4,79,26
Duty at 30%		
Silk Piecegoods etc.		88,22
Others		96,02
Special Duties (Discriminating between British and Non-British Manufacture)		
Iron & Steel		
British Manufactures		44,73
Non-British Manufactures *with* extra duty		1,08,42
Non-British Manufactures *without* extra duty		1,71,41
Paper and Stationery		26,92
Railway Plant and Rolling Stock (Government)		27,93
Others		50,54
Total Revenue from Imports		40,46,17
Sea Customs — Exports		
		In Thousands of Rs.
Hides & Skins		37,33
Jute : Raw		2,18,69
: Manufactured		2,41,28
Rice		1,06,54
Tea		1,33
Government Stores		3
Total Revenue from Exports		6,05,20
		In Thousands of Rs.
Sea Customs—Miscellaneous		14,42
Land Customs		27,80
Excise Duty : Motor Spirit	1,21,23	
Kerosene	97,81	2,18,41
Warehouse & Wharf Rent		47
Miscellaneous		5,21
		2,66,31
Revenue from Imports		40,46,17
Revenue from Exports		6,05,20
		4,917,68

less Refunds	96,27
	48,21,41
less Charges	84,81
Net Yield from Customs in thousands of Rs.	47,36,60

V. EXPENDITURE ON DEFENCE

A comparative study of 41 Nations.

The following table is adapted from a reproduction in *New India* of 17th April 1930 "with certain changes in the order of the countries and with the omission of certain details, from Mr. Arnold J. Toynbee's 'Survey of International Affairs'. The information contained in the table has been taken by him from 'The Armaments Year Book' of the League of Nations".

Country	Year	Equivalent in Pounds Sterling	Per cent to total Expenditure
India (not including Debt Services)	1927–28	42,617,535	45.29
China		20,592,188	43.13
Poland (excludes Pensions & Debt Service)	1927–28	13,848,888	31.58
Portugal (includes Pensions & some Civil Expense)	1926–27	4,437,146	27.39
Japan	1927–28	47,235,969	26.57
Spain	1927	25,589,770	25.97
Switzerland	1927–28	3,383,758	25.83
Latvia	1927–28	1,621,301	25.12
Italy	1927–28	45,895,140	23.46
Esthonia	1927–28	1,022,880	23.46
Chile	1927	5,356,624	23.32
Mexico (excludes Pensions)	1927	7,536,271	23.02
Greece (excludes Pensions and Debt Services)	1927–28	5,017,784	21.92
France („ „ „)	1927	63,368,635	19.75
Jugoslavia („ „ „)	1926–27	8,742,753	19.29
Lithuania	1927	801,829	19.05
Bolivia	1925	590,612	19.03
Sweden	1927–28	7,597,027	18.79

Peru	1927	1,433,766	18.63
Argentina (excludes Pensions and Debt Services)	1926	21,596,545	18.19
Bulgaria	1927–28	1,830,080	17.79
Brazil (excludes Debt Service)	1927	7,723,373	17.52
Czecho-Slovakia (excludes Pension and Debt Service)	1927	10,274,390	17.36
Uruguay	1925–26	1,544,248	17.07
United States of America (excludes Pension and Debt Service)	1927–28	1,20,178,130	16.09
Soviet Russia	1925–26	64,427,055	16.01
Finland (excludes Pension and Debt Service)	1927	3,118,082	15.91
Ecuador (excludes Pensions)	1927	314,026	15.88
Cuba („ „)	1927–28	2,537,052	15.05
*GREAT BRITAIN & NORTHERN IRELAND	1927–28	120,695,000	14.75
Netherlands (excludes Debt Service)	1927	7,848,309	13.06
Denmark (excludes Pensions and Debt Service)	1927–28	2,225,279	12.79
Norway (excludes Debt Service)	1927–28	2,214,137	10.31
Hungary („ „)	1926–27	3,989,935	9.7
*IRISH FREE STATE	1927–28	2,480,000	7.69
Belgium (excludes Pensions and Debt Service)	1927	3,480,080	7.67
Germany (excludes Pensions and Debt Service)	1927-28	33,137,384	7.16
*AUSTRALIA	1926–27	5,556,000	6.52
Austria	1927	2,318,061	6.37
*NEW ZEALAND (excludes Pensions & Debt Service)	1927–28	958,321	3.91
*UNION OF SOUTH AFRICA (excludes Pensions & Debt Service)	1927–28	1,125,900	3.16

It will be noticed that India leads the list while the rest of the British Empire brings up the rear.

APPENDIX E

Congress Select Committee on the Financial Obligations between Great Britain and India

At The Karachi Congress, the Working Committee appointed a Select Committee consisting of Sjt. D. N. Bahadurji, Prof. K. T. Shah, Sjts. Bhulabhai J. Desai and J. C. Kumarappa (convener) to carry out a scrutiny into the financial transactions of the East India Company and the British Government in India and the so-called Public Debt of India, and to report on the obligations which should, in future, be borne by India or England. We give below a summary of their report.

I. SUMMARY

The report is divided into three main parts. First it scrutinizes the totality of the transactions of the East India Company up to 1858, then the financial obligations since the transfer of the government to the Crown, dividing the obligations into (a) debts that are not backed by any assets, and (b) debts which have created or left some material assets, and lastly it gives its recommendations.

It is argued that during the whole period of the British rule no burden has been undertaken by the Government of India with the assent of the people, and that therefore at this time it is necessary to examine such burdens with reference to their justice and propriety. It is also pointed out that "Public Debt" in India is not a " National Debt " for it is the result of the acts of the representatives of the British Nation as India had not even the " shadow of a constitution ". However, the report recognizes the fact that debts " incurred justly and for the benefit of the people of India " should be taken over by India.

UNDER THE REGIME OF THE EAST INDIA COMPANY

The history of the East India Company is sketched briefly to trace the transformation of a trading concern into a territorial power within two centuries. As the accounts of the territorial and commercial sides of the East India Company were mixed up hopelessly, the Committee accept as the starting point the amount of debt of the Company as at 30th April 1857, immediately before the Mutiny, at the figure contained in the return of the Debt presented to Parliament in 1881 on the motion of Sir George Balfour. This stands at £ 51 millions. This is accounted for in the main by a few transactions as follows, in round figures :

External Wars of the Company :	
1st Afghan War	15 millions
Two Burmese Wars	14 ,,
Expeditions to China, Persia, Nepal, etc.	6 ,,
Interest paid on the East India Company's Capital etc., 1833-1857	15 ,,
	£ 50 millions

EXTERNAL WARS OF THE COMPANY

As regards the equity of charging the cost of the external wars, the following quotation from Sir George Wingate is of interest :

"Most of our Asiatic Wars with countries beyond the limits of our Empire have been carried on by means of the Military and monetary resources of the Government of India though the objects of these wars were in some instances purely British, and in others but remotely connected with the interests of India. They were undertaken by the Government of India in obedience to instructions received from the British Ministries of the time acting through the Presidents of the Board of Control; and for all consequence they have involved, the British Nation is clearly responsible. The Afghan War was one of the most notable of these, and it is now well understood that this war was undertaken by the British Government without consulting the Court of Directors, and in opposition to their views. It was, in fact, a purely British War, but notwithstanding this, and in defiance of a solemn expression of unanimous opinion on the part of the Court of Directors, and of a resolution of the Court of Proprietors of the East India Company that the whole cost of the war should not be thrown upon the Indian finances, the Ministry required this to be done. By this injustice, ten millions were added to the debt of India. The late Persian War proclaimed by the British Ministry in pursuance of a policy with which India had no real concern ; the war, nevertheless, was carried on by the troops and resources of India, and one half only of the total cost was subsequently settled to be borne by the revenues of this country. India, in fact, has been required to furnish men and means for carrying on all our Asiatic Wars and has never, in any instance, been paid a full equivalent for the assistance thus rendered which furnishes irrefragable proof of the one-sided and selfish character of our Indian policy."

This is supported by John Bright, who said in the House of Commons:

"Last year I referred to the enormous expenses of the Afghan War the real burden of which ought to be thrown on the taxation of the people of England, because it was recommended by the English Cabinet for objects supposed to be English."

It is recommended that this £ 35 million should be borne by Great Britain.

COMPANY'S CAPITAL REDEMPTION ETC.

The East India Company's Stock of £ 6 million was redeemed at a premium in 1874 by a payment of £ 12 million and interest had been paid at 10% under the terms of the Chartered Act of 1833. These payments aggregate to over £ 37 million as follows:

Interest payments	1833–1857	15,120,000
,, ,,	1858–1874	10,080,000
Capital Stock		12,000,000
		£ 37,200,000

In the words of the report, "as against this charge upon the revenues of India, India received no substantial benefit. It practically amounts to the purchase price paid to the East India Company for the surrender of such rights and properties as they may have had in the trade of India and for such properties as they then possessed. The actual charge was the outcome of the arrangement made between the East India Company's Directors and Proprietors on the one hand, and the British Government representing the British Parliament and the British Public, on the other. In this the Indian people had absolutely no say, nor had their interests any consideration whatsoever. This arrangement cannot, in equity and good conscience, be held to be binding on the Indian people. India, as already mentioned, received no benefit from the transactions between the British Government and the Company's Directors, either in the shape of the assets claimed to be valuable and surrendered by the Company or in the tangible form of any special advantage such as that which results from having sole charge of one's country's government; or even from having a fair share of the opportunities of service and development of the country's resources. Indians were denied these privileges in their own country all through the Company's rule. The British Government, on the other hand, received many a considerable, as well as valuable, advantage from the operations of the East India Company, both as a territorial and a commercial body."

COST OF THE "MUTINY"

The next claim is in respect of £ 40 million, the cost of the "Mutiny" of 1857. As these operations were necessitated "by the mismanagement and misgovernment of India by those who were in charge of it, the British Government, for whom the Company was carrying on the Government of India at the time, is necessarily the proper party to shoulder that burden." The following extract from the letter of the Secretary of State for India dated 8th August 1872 is given in support of this claim:

> "The extraordinary case of the great Mutiny of 1857-58 is the only case which gives even plausibility to the war office representation; in that case, altogether unprecedented in the history of British India, the Imperial Government was compelled, under the imminent risk of losing its Empire in the East, to make one of those efforts which are at times inseparable from Imperial power and Imperial obligations. It must be remembered, however, that, if similar exertions had been called for by war in any other part of Her Majesty's dominions, not only must the same effort have been made, but the burden of it must necessarily have been borne, in greater part, at least, by the Imperial Government; but in regard to the Indian Munity, no part of the cost of suppressing it was allowed to fall on the Imperial Exchequer: the whole of it was or is now being defrayed by the Indian taxpayer."

The case of the Boer struggle is referred to as an instance where this principle was acted on. In that case Britain not only bore the cost of the war herself but also paid £ 3 million to assist the Boers to restore devastated farms.

"Thus the burdens and obligations which have fallen upon the people of India from the East India Company amount to over 112 million sterling made up as follows:

Cost of the first Afghan War	15,000,000
,, ,, ,, two Burmese Wars	14,000,000
,, ,, ,, Expeditions to China, Persia, etc.	6,000,000

On account of Company's Capital and Dividend	37,200,000
Cost of the Mutiny	40,000,000
	£ 112,200,000

"It is but fair that India should now claim to be relieved from the burdens of expenditures which were wrongly put on her shoulders."

INDIA UNDER THR BRITISH CROWN

The financial transactions of the Government of India since 1858 have been considered in two sections: (a) those in regard to obligations described as "Unproductive", in which group come in items such as the Cost of External Wars, Miscellaneous Charges, Famine Relief Charges, Exchange Losses, etc.

EXTERNAL WARS

Expenses aggregating to over 37 crores in connection with the Abyssinian Expedition, Second Afghan War, Military operations in Egypt and North West Frontier, the Burmese War etc. are challenged on the ground that these were all undertaken in Imperial interest, that is to say, in the interest of Great Britain, and India was not concerned in them at all. In support of this contention is cited the statements of Lord Salisbury, Lord Northbrooke, the Secretary of State for India, Sir Charles Trevelyan, Lord Lytton, Messrs. Fawcett, Gladstone, Gokhale, Sir. D. E. Wachha and others.

As regards the European War (1914-1918), claims under two heads are made: (1) The return of the War "Gifts", and (2) a share of the War Cost. The first claim amounting to 189 crores is made on two grounds:

(a) That the Government of India, under the Statutes by which it is regulated, had no power whatsoever to make a gift to Great Britain out of the revenues of India, and therefore the "Gifts", being illegal transactions, should be returned.

(b) The amount was beyond the financial ability of the people of India, and that India had contributed, apart from these financial "Gifts", by way of men and material far in excess of the contribution of any of the Dominions.

The second claim in respect of part of the cost of the Military operations amounts to 171 crores. This is arrived at by adopting as Standard Military expenditure the amount spent in the year 1914-15, and the excess over such Standard between 1915-16 to 1920-21 is claimed.

Thus, under this head of "External Wars," a claim of over 397 crores is made.

MISCELLANEOUS CHARGES

The expenses incurred in the maintenance of India Office, Aden, Persian and Chinese Consulates, Ecclesiastical Charges, etc., estimated at £ 20 million, are challenged on the ground that these are Imperial charges, and so should fall on the Imperial Exchequer and not on India. Here, again, the claim is supported by the opinions of Maj. Gen. Collon, Mr. Stephen Jacob, C. S. I., the Welby Commission etc.

BURMAH

It is claimed that the deficits of Burmah budgets since 1886, aggregating to about 15 crores and the interest charges and Railway deficits of about 22 crores and a share in respect of the expenses of Indian defence calculated at one crore a year amounting to 45 crores for the period since 1886, aggregating in all to 82 crores, should be made good to India. (One member of the Committee is of the view that the claim in respect of Burmah should not be made except in the event of that province being separated.)

FAMINE RELIEF CHARGES

Expenses and burdens imposed by these measures are recommended to be borne by India as these were incurred in her interest, however wastefully it might have been administered.

EXCHANGE LOSSES

It is pointed out that the country has suffered incalculable damage both in regard to its trade and as regards the depreciation of its silver wealth as a consequence of the exchange and currency policy of the Government. No claim is, however, suggested, and the losses are looked upon "as the price India has had to pay for the general financial incompetence and mismanagement" of its administrators.

REVERSE COUNCILS

This is described as the "most lamentable" operation, and the losses resulting from these transactions, amounting to about 35 crores, it is claimed, should be made good by Great Britain.

RAILWAYS

The policy of encouraging Railway construction by the system of Guaranteeing Interest on the Capital sunk has led to considerable waste, and in many cases the cost per mile of a Guaranteed Railway is double that of a State-built Railway. This extravagance is strongly criticized. Many or most of the Railways were built out of Military considerations, and only of late they have been able to pay their way. Strictly, a considerable amount of this so-called "developmental" expenditure should be charged to Military expenditures. Be it as it may, the recommendation confines itself to only the expenses of admittedly strategic lines in the N. W. F. Province and at Aden costing about 33 crores, which should be paid by Great Britain.

When the Railway properties were acquired by the State, the acquisition was made under conditions that added considerably to the burdens of the people. The Companies were entitled, under the terms of their Contracts, to be paid the market value of their Shares or Stock, at the date of acquisition. Because of the Guaranteed Interest payments the Market Price of these Stocks and Shares went up enormously when the State was about to acquire the properties. The Companies thus obtained a high price which was not warranted by their assets or by the return from their revenues. This is an unjustifiable burden to be imposed on the people of India amounting to about 50 crores.

It is further pointed out that the fixed rate of exchange provided in the Contracts of the Railway Companies occasioned enormous losses to Indian revenue, but the actual amount of loss is difficult of determination, and the Committee submits that a deduction on this account must be made before taking over the debt said to be incurred on Railway account.

As regards the other "Productive" debt items such as Irrigation, Posts & Telegraphs, etc., no claim is suggested although the extravagance of building a new Capital at Delhi is criticized and the Back Bay Reclamation scheme in Bombay is condemned.

Thus the total claims advanced are as follows :

	Crores	Crores
Under the Company		
External Wars	35	
Capital & Interest	37	
Cost of Mutiny	40	112
Under the British Crown		
External Wars	37	
European War : "Gifts"	189	
Cost	171	397
Miscellaneous Charges		20
In respect of Burmah		82
Reverse Council Losses		35
Railways		83
Total Rs.		729 crores

(Exchange 2/- to 1900 and 1/4 since)

RECOMMENDATIONS

The present "Public Debt" of India amounts to over, 1,100 crores. Taking into consideration the ever-growing material and political gain to Great Britain as the result of possessing India, and in consideration of the suppression of Indian industries and talents, the Committee recommends that Great Britain should follow in dealing with India the precedent she set in releasing Ireland of her share of the national debt of the United Kingdom when Ireland was made a Free State. "Every principle of fair play now requires that, if India is to start on a new era of National Self-government, it should start freely and without any burden, if any progress is to be achieved at all. India cannot afford to bear any additional taxation. The only possibilities of progress for India, therefore, are in the application of the national revenues to national purposes, and it is only by reducing the national expenditure on the civil and military administration of the country to suit its own requirements and freeing India from the liabilities for the public debts not incurred in her interests, that saving can be effected which would be applicable to the advancement of India in the matter of education and sanitation and other national means of regeneration."

II. Annual Military Expenditures

(A Note by J. C. Kumarappa)

In addition to the claims made in our unanimous Report, I wish to put before the Working Committee the following note on Annual Military Expenditures for their consideration. This claim has been suggested in the last sentence of the 52nd paragraph of the Report.

Annual Military Expenditure — It is a notorious fact that the bulk of our revenues have been spent on the primary functions of government. In a list of military expenditure of 41 nations prepared in 1929 by Mr. A. J. Toynbee in "Survey of International Affairs", India stands first with 45.29 per cent of her expenditures being military expenditures. The rank according to the ratio of military expenditure to total expenditures and that ratio are also given below in respect of the principal militaristic countries of the world:

		Percentage of Expenditures
1st	India	45.29
5th	Japan	26.57
9th	Italy	23.46
14th	France	19.75
25th	U. S. A.	16.09
30th	Great Britain	14.75
37th	Germany	7.16

It will be noticed that India's proportion is more than three times that of Great Britain. This is not the place to go into the damage caused to the country by starving nation-building expenditures to find the wherewithal for the military expenditures. But it must be observed that the army in India since 1857 has been in the nature of an army of occupation. The proportion of European to Indian troops has been increased since that date from 1 to 5 to the present ratio of 1 to 2 to assure the safety of British occupation. That the strength of the Indian army has been maintained at a high level for Imperial purposes is obvious from the fact that whenever Indian troops were required for Imperial Wars outside India, they were taken away for varying periods without any hesitation and without any attempt to replace them during their absence from India. India has thus been used "as a barrack in the Eastern Seas" for providing troops for British Imperial purposes. As the cost of each European soldier is estimated to be about 3 to 4 times the cost of an Indian sepoy, the military expenditure of the Government of India has been considerably in excess of what it need have been, if the army was maintained merely for defence and internal order and consisted purely of sepoys. Such being the case, that amount of the expenditure representing the excess over the needs of India, should be legitimately borne by Great Britain.

Apart from this, Imperial considerations have led to the keeping up of a much higher standard of equipment etc., than would have been required by purely local needs. Mr. Buchanan, a member of the Welby Commission, says in his reservation No. 4 to the Report of the Commission :

"It has already been pointed out that, in so far as the military defence of India is concerned, India pays everything, and the United Kingdom nothing. And yet the maintenance of the military defence of India is one of the greatest of Imperial questions.

"The military strength of India is the main factor in the strength of our Empire in the East. In virtue of that strength Great Britain is a great Asiatic power. We have had overwhelming practical evidence of the value to the Empire of the military forces of India in the aid, both direct and indirect, which she is rendering to us in the South African War. Nearly 6,000 British troops on complete war footing were rapidly despatched at a critical moment from India to Natal, others have followed, and Indian Native regiments now garrison Mauritius, Ceylon, Singapore, and other places from which British troops have been withdrawn for the purposes of the war.

"Surely, therefore, both on general grounds and from our recent experience of the efficient help that India's military strength can give to the Empire, it is established beyond question that India's strength is the Empire's strength, and that in discharging these Imperial duties India has a fair claim that part of the burden should be borne by the Imperial Exchequer. There may be difficulties as to the method of making the charge and the amount; as to the equity of the claim on the part of India there can be no doubt."

(*Indian Expenditure Commission* 1895, Vol. IV, p. 149).

In the financial statement of 1885-6, para 136, the then Finance Minister, Sir Auckland Colvin, estimated the net cost of the army (exclusive of cost of wars) at about £ 15 million or without exchange at fifteen crores of rupees every year.

" This amount," he said, " may be considered to be about the normal military expenditure in India and England." This gives an Indian Government Standard for Military Expenditures, which has to be adjusted for variation in price levels. Until 1900, the variation in the Price Index was very little, taking the year 1873 as base year. The figure for 1910 was 122, and for 1915 it was 152, and at present it is about 200. Allowing for these variations, the following standards may be used for the period indicated :

1859/60 — 1900 a standard of	15 crores a year.	
1900 — 1915 with increase of $33\frac{1}{3}$ per cent.	20 ,,	,,
1915 — 1931 with increase of 100 ,,	30 ,,	,,

This method of arriving at a standard, however unsatisfactory, does not deviate far from facts is shown by its approximating to actual expenditures. In 1875, the expenditure was 14.66 crores, while the standard is fifteen crores. Similarly in 1915, the actual expenditure was 30.80 crores, while the standard is 30 crores. Although it may be held that even these standards are far too high, yet accepting them, for argument's sake, the standard expenditure for the whole period will be—

Standard Military Expenditure

		Crores	Crores
1859/60 — 1899/1900 @ 15 crores	40 × 15	600	
1900/01 — 1914/15 ,, 20 ,,	15 × 20	300	
1915/16 — 1930/31 ,, 30 ,,	16 × 30	480	1380
Actual expenditure for the whole period 1859—1930 as per list appended . . .			2128.33
Less Standard as above . . .			1380.00
		Balance	748.33
Less items, subject of separate claim in respect of Wars, 1860-1900, say . .	37.5 crores		
,, European War	170.7 ,,		208.20
Excessive military expenditure caused by maintaining the Indian army for Imperial purposes which ought to have been borne by Great Britain.		(Crores) Rs.	540.13

ANNUAL NET MILITARY EXPENDITURES

Detailed List referred to in Note 1

The figures for the years 1859/60—1920/21 are taken from K. T. Shah's *Sixty Years of Indian Finance* which were themselves obtained from Government statements. The figures for 1921/22 to 1928/29 are taken from the statistical abstracts and the last two years from the *Gazette of India*, 11th April 1931. The amounts are in crores.

Year		
1859–60	19.38	19.38
1860–1	16.47	
1861–2	13.25	
1862–3	12.52	
1863–4	12.21	
1864–5	12.71	
1865–6	13.53	
1866–7	12.08	
1867–8	12.33	
1868–9	15.58	
1869–70	16.20	136.88
1870–1	15.54	
1871–2	15.11	
1872–3	14.64	
1873–4	14.45	
1874–5	13.69	
1875–6	14.66	
1876–7	15.32	
1877–8	17.72	
1878–9	18.32	
1879–80	22.29	161.74
1880–1	27.59	
1881–2	16.96	
1882–3	18.08	
1883–4	17.99	
1884–5	17.36	
1885–6	20.09	

Year		
1886–7	21.21	
1887–8	21.12	
1888–9	21.12	
1889–90	21.56	202.08
1890–1	21.61	
1891–2	24.54	
1892–3	23.98	
1893–4	24.32	
1894–5	25.73	120.18
1895–6	25.39	
1896–7	24.56	
1897–8	27.03	
1898–9	24.31	
1899–1900	23.07	124.36
1900–1	23.21	
1901–2	24.24	
1902–3	26.45	
1903–4	27.21	
1904–5	31.04	
1905–6	29.51	
1906–7	30.25	
1907–8	28.87	
1908–9	29.40	
1909–10	28.66	278.84
1910–1	31.89	
1911–2	29.33	

1912–3	29.34		1922–3	65.26	
1913–4	29.84		1923–4	56.52	
1914–5	30.80		1924–5	55.63	
1915–6	33.39		1925–6	55.99	
1916–7	37.48		1926–7	55.97	
1917–8	43.56		1927–8	54.79	
1918–9	66.72		1928–9	55.10	
1919–20	86.97	419.32	1929–30	55.10	611.25
1920–1	87.38		1930–31 R. E.		54.30
1921–2	69.81				
			Total (Crores) Rs.		2128.33

III. INTEREST PAYMENTS ON CLAIMS

(A Note by J. C. Kumarappa)

In addition to the claims made in our unanimous Report, I wish to put before the Working Committee the following note on Interest Payments on Claims for their consideration.

Interest Payments on Claims—As regards the items of non-productive expenditure objected to in the Report which were represented by interest-bearing debts, all principles of business practice demand that where an item has been wrongly debited and interest payments have been made on account of these debits, such interest amounts should be made good. If the original debit to India is proved to be wrong, then it is but right to demand restitution of all payments made in respect of such a debit.

It should be borne in mind that in claiming these Interest payments, a claim is made not for a consequential loss but for an actual loss. In such a case the Interest payments themselves are Principals which have been erroneously paid and hence the claims in respect thereof.

These interest payments would have fallen on the British Exchequer, had the original debit been placed on the right shoulders. The British Exchequer has been relieved to that extent and hence this claim only amounts to asking the party, who should have originally paid it, to pay it now. Strict commercial practice will allow of not merely the simple interest paid but also interest on such payments, that is in effect compound interest. But the claim now made is only for a refund of what has actually been taken out of the Indian Exchequer.

The Interest Payments have been annual payments, and hence a claim extending over seventy years would more than turn over the original debit three times. But this cannot be helped as the annual charges have been persistently made in the face of many challenges of the original charge by Britishers themselves. When a similar cumulative claim was made by Mr. Gokhale before the Welby Commission, and when that was objected to, Mr. Gokhale replied:

> "It is the natural way of looking at the thing for those who think a charge is unjust."

The rate of interest on Government Loans has varied from time to time from 3½ per cent to 7 per cent, and it is difficult to determine the rate that should be claimed. The average rate on all Government loans works out at 4 per cent, and it is submitted that a charge to Great Britain at 4 per cent simple interest on those items cannot be considered unreasonable. Interest is so calculated on the following items from the dates when the obligations were imposed except as to item No 4; Interest on item No. 4 is calculated from 1880 as bulk of the obligations which aggregate to 37.5 crores were created between 1878 and 1886.

				Interest
1. E. I. Company's wars	35	Crores	1857-1931	103.60
2. Cost of "Mutiny"	40	,,	1860-1931	113.60
3. E. I. Company's Capital and Interest	37	,,	1874-1931	84.36
4. External Wars since 1857	37.5	,,	1880-1931	76.50
5. European War Cost	17.9	,,	1920-1931	157.96
Gift	18.9	,,		
			Total (Crores) Rs.	536.02

Though it is not possible at the present time to trace into the schedule of Public Debts the debts of which a refund is claimed, one is able, by collating the Amount of Claims, the Public Debt and the Interest paid thereon at a particular period, to show that the amount of Interest paid is practically on the

Principal amounts for which a refund is claimed. This fact is brought out in the following table, which also shows that the rate claimed, 4 per cent, is reasonable. The amounts are given in crores of rupees :

Year	*Amount of our claim*	*Public Debt*	*Interest paid during the year*
1860	75.0	9.30	4.2
1874	112.0	117.0	5.3
1880	149.5	157.3	6.9
1890	149.5	207.1	9.3
1900	149.5	307.6	11.1
1910	149.5	405.6	14.25
1920	508.5	544.1	31.9
1931	508.5	Over 1100.0	50.14 R. E.

The total interest paid works out as follows :

1860-1874	81.0
1875-1900	226.5
1901-1920	326.8
1921-1931	415.4
Total paid Crores Rs.	1049.7

So that our claim amounts, in effect, to asking for a refund of interest amounting to Rs. 536 crores out of a payment of Rs. 1050 crores unjustly paid out of the revenues of India in relief of the British Exchequer.

BIBLIOGRAPHY

ADAMS, Brooks *The Law of Civilization and Decay*, New York, Macmillan, 1921.

AMBEDKAR, B. R. *The Problem of the Rupee*, London, King and Son, 1923.

ANSTEY, VERA *The Economic Development of India*, London, Longmans Green and Co., 1929.

BADEN-POWELL, B. H. *Land Systems of British India*, Oxford, Clarendon Press, 1892. *Land Revenue in British India*, Oxford, Clarendon Press, 1913.

BALKRISHNA *Commercial Relations between England and India*, London, Routledge, 1924.

BANERJEE P. *A Study of Indian Economics*, London, Macmillan and Co. *Indian Finance in Days of the Company*, Macmillan and Co., 1928. *Provincial Finance in India*, Macmillan and Co., 1929. *A History of Indian Taxation*, Macmillan and Co., 1930.

BLUNT, W. S. *India under Ripon*, London, T. and F. Unwin, 1909.

COYAJEE, J. C. *Indian Fiscal Problem*, Patna, Patna University, 1924.

DAVENPORT, H. J. *Economics of Enterprise*, New York, Macmillan, 1925.

DUBEY, D. L. *The Indian Public Debt*, Bombay, Taraporewalla and Son, 1930.

DIGBY, WM. *Ruining of India : Indian Problem for English Consideration : 'Prosperous' British India*, London, Unwin, 1901.

DUTT, R. C. *Economic History of India*, 1902, *India under Early British Rule*, *India in the Victorian Age*, London, Kegan, Paul, Trench. *Famines in India*, Truberner and Co., 1906.

GADGIL, D. R. *The Industrial Evolution of India*, London, Milford, 1924.

GHOSE, S. C. *Indian Railway Rates*, Government Press, 1918. *Lectures on Indian Railway Economics.*

HAMILTON, C. J. *Trade Relations between England and India*, Calcutta, Thacker Spink, 1919.

HAMILTON, SIR D. *India-Her Present and Future*, Calcutta, *Calcutta Review* 1916.

HEBER, BISHOP *Journal of Travels.*

HOBSON, J. A. *Work and Wealth*, London, Macmillan, 1916.

HOLLAND, W. E. S. *The Indian Outlook*, London, Edinburgh House Press, 1917.

HOWARD, H. F. *India and Gold Standard*, Calcutta, Thacker Spink, 1911.

HUNTER, SIR WM. *The India of the Queen and Other Essays*, 1903.

HYNDMAN, H. M. *Bankruptcy of India*, 1888; *The Truth About India.*

IYER, K. V. *Indian Railways*, London, Milford, 1924.

JEVONS, H. S. *Exchange and Indian Currency*, London, Milford, 1922.

KALE, V. G. *Indian Industrial and Economic Problems*, Madras, Natesan. *Gokhale and Economic Reforms*, Poona, Aryabhushan Press. *Indian Economics, 6th Ed.* Poona, Aryabhushan Press, 1917.

KUMARAPPA, J. C. *A Survey of Matar Taluka*, Ahmedabad, Navajivan Press, 1931.

LAJPAT RAI *England's Debt to India*, New York, B. W. Huebsch, 1917.
Unhappy India, Calcutta, Banna Publishing Co., 1928.

LOVEDAY A. *History and Economics of Indian Famines*, London, Bell, 1914.

LUTZ H. L. *Public Finance*, New York, Appleton, 1925.

MACAULAY, LORD *Essays & Biographies*, London, Longmans Green and Co.

MAC DONALD, J. R. *The Awakening of India*, London, Hodder & Stoughton, 1910. *The Government of India*, London, Viking, 1920.

MARSHALL, A. *Industry and Trade*, London, Macmillan, 1920.

MATTHAI, JOHN *Village Government in British India*, London, Fisher Unwin, 1915.

MEHTA, N. B. *Indian Railways : Rates and Regulations*, London, P. S. King and Son, 1927.

MOOKERJI, RADHAKUMUD *A History of Indian Shipping*, New York, Longmans, 1927.

MUKERJI, RADHAKAMAL *Foundations of Indian Economics*, New York, Longmans Green, 1916. *Principles of Comparative Economics* London, P. S. King and Son, 1922. *Borderlands of Economics*, London, Allen and Unwin, 1925. *The Rural Economy of India*, New York, Longman, 1926.

PAUL, K. T. *The British Connection with India*, London, Student Christian Movement, 1927.

PECK, H. W. *Taxation and Welfare*, New York, Macmillan, 1925.

PILLAI, P. *Economic Conditions in India*, London, Routledge, 1925.

RANADE, M. G. *Essays on Indian Economics*, Madras, Natesan, 1916.

RUTHERFORD, V. H. *Modern India*, London, Labour Publishing Co., 1927.

SAMADDAR, J. N. *The Economic Condition of Ancient India*, Calcutta University, 1922.

SELIGMAN, E. R. A. *Studies in Public Finance*, 1925. *Essays in Taxation*, 1925. *The Shifting and Incidence of Taxation*, 1927.

SHAH, K. T. *Sixty Years of Indian Finance*, 2nd *Ed.; Trade, Tariffs and Transport in India*, 1923.

,, AND KHAMBATTA *The Wealth & Taxable Capacity of India*, London, King and Son, 1925.

SHIRRAS, G. F. *Indian Finance and Banking*, London, Macmillan, 1920. *Report on an Enquiry into Working Class Budgets in Bombay*, Government Central Press, 1923. *The Science of Public Finance*, London, Macmillan, 1925.

SMITH, H. B. LEES *India and the Tariff Problem*, London, Constable, 1909.

VAKIL, C. N. *Our Fiscal Policy*, Bombay, Taraporewalla, 1923. *Financial Developments in Modern India*, London, King & Son, 1924.

VAKIL, C. N. and MURANJAN *Currency and Prices in India*, London, King and Son, 1927.

VISVESVARAYA, Sir M. *Reconstructing India*, London, King and Son, 1920.

WACHA, D. E. *Indian Railway Finance*, Madras, Natesan, 1912.

WADIA, P. A. *The Wealth of India*, London, Macmillan, 1925.

WADIA P. A. AND JOSHI *Money and Money Market in India*, London, Macmillan, 1926.

WILLIAMS, RUSHBROOK *India in* 1923-24.

YUSUF ALI, A. *The Making of India*, London, Black, 1925.

Cost of Government in the United States.
National Industrial Conference Board.

The report of the Congress Select Committee on the Financial Obligations between Great Britain & India,
Bombay, 1931.

The Report of the Indian Fiscal Commission : 1921-22.

The Statistical Abstract of British India.

Statesman's Year Book.

The Indian Economic Journal, Allahabad.

The Mysore Journal of Economics, Bangalore City.

Minutes of Evidence on the Affairs of the East India Company.

GLOSSARY OF SOME TECHNICAL TERMS

Direct Taxes are those which are intended to be borne by the persons on whom they are levied.

Indirect Taxes are levied on one set of persons in the expectation and intention that they will be passed on to others by the process of shifting.

The Source of Taxation is the fund or flow of wealth from which all taxes are paid — Property and income.

Proportional or Uniform Taxation is the same for all amounts as the rate is constant irrespective of the tax base.

Progressive: rates are increased as the amount assessed increases.

Regressive: size of rate diminishes as the assessed amount increases.

Degressive: when taxed amount is subject to abatements and exemptions to a certain limit.

Faculty: ability of the citizen to bear the burden of Government as represented by taxes both direct and indirect and expenses of public undertakings.

INDEX

BY THE SAME AUTHOR

1. **Christianity — Its Economy and Way of Life**

   This booklet presents a critical approach to the practice of the Church and discusses even political and economic problems such as democracy, government, planned economy, production, consumption etc., in relation to true Christian life.

2. **Why the Village Movement ?**

   Gandhiji says: " Prof. J. C. Kumarappa answers about all the doubts that have been expressed about the necessity and feasibility of the movement. No lover of villages can afford to be without the booklet. No doubter can fail to have his doubts dispelled. . . . I wonder if the village movement has come just in time to prevent the spread of the movement of despair. This booklet is an attempt to answer the question."

3. **The Economy of Permanence**

   Gandhiji says: " When I took up the manuscript I was curious to know what it could contain. The opening chapter satisfied my curiosity and led me on to the end without fatigue and yet with profit."

4. **Practice & Precepts of Jesus**

   Gandhiji says: " Having carefully gone through these chapters, I can recommend their perusal to every believer in God, be he a Christian or a follower of any other religion . . . It is a revolutionary view of Jesus as a man of God . . . If all believe, as Prof. Kumarappa does, there will be no religious feuds and rivalries between sects and sects and different religions."

   The Missionary Journal " Dnanodaya " says:

   " We trust our readers will not fail to pray that the Spirit of Christ who led Prof. Kumarappa to write it will bless its many readers . . . to read it is a searching spiritual exercise . . . The shining sincerity reflected on every page of this book makes it a benediction to read."

5. **A Survey of Matar Taluka** (Dealing with the economic condition of about 60 villages of Gujarat)

   Kakasaheb Kalelkar writes: " The report is presented to the public as an authoritative document on the economic condition of a typical taluka of Gujarat. The reader will find that the statistics presented here in careful schedules are even more eloquent than the main body of the carefully worded and lucid report itself. It is a vivid picture of the slow process of exploitation, emasculation and perhaps decimating of a patient and peaceful population."

6. **Planned Economy** (A Gandhian Approach)

7. A Plan for the Economic Development of N. W. F. Province

Sir Mirza Ismail writes: "I should like to compliment you on the very lucid manner in which you have dealt with the various questions relating to the industrial development of the province. You have approached the whole problem in a direct matter-of-fact and eminently practical way."

8. Organization and Accounts of Relief Work

Dr. Rajendra Prasad says: "This pamphlet summarizes and collects and collates our experience and method of work (in Bihar Earthquake Relief) and Shri J. C. Kumarappa has done a public service in bringing together the points which may appear obvious now, but which were not so obvious when we started, and which needed much thought to make them clear. I hope it will prove helpful not only to new organizations engaged in similar work but also to students and would-be organizers and social workers."

9. Currency Inflation : Cause and Cure

10. Clive to Keynes

This is a short survey of the history of India's Public Debts and Credits. It is replete with facts and figures which make the author's thesis convincing.

With the Author as Chairman :

The C. P. Government Industrial Survey Committee Report

Gandhiji writes: "Chapter 2 dealing with general considerations stamps the report as an original document and shows that it is not to be pigeon-holed as most such reports are but should be given effect to without delay."

"The committee has made practical suggestions on all the industries. The curious must procure the report and study it."

Part I Vol. 1. pp. 50

General recommendations to Government based on a survey of 606 villages.

,, I Vol. 2. Section I, pp. 82

Two selected District Survey reports

,, I Vol. 2. Section II, pp. 103

Notes on 24 Village Industries

,, II Vol. I. pp. 40

Recommendations in regard to forests, mineral, and power resources.

,, II Vol. II

Selected portions on reports on forests, mineral, power resources and on transport, taxation and marketing.

With the Author as Convener of a Congress Select Committee :

The financial obligations between Great Britain and India.

(These and other books are available from the Secretary, A. I. V. I. A., Maganvadi, Wardha, C. P.)